Life, Lies, & Second Chances

Life, Lies, & Second Chances
Developing Resilience to Overcome Adversity

Robby S. Fakhouri

All Rights Reserved. No portion of this book may be reproduced, stored in a retrieval system, or transmitted in any form or by any means – electronic, mechanical, photocopy, recording, scanning, or other – except for brief quotations in critical reviews or articles without the prior permission of the author.

Published by Game Changer Publishing

Paperback ISBN: 978-1-962656-72-6
Hardcover ISBN: 978-1-962656-76-4
Digital: ISBN: 978-1-962656-74-0

www.GameChangerPublishing.com

DEDICATION

Courage. It's a big word with big responsibilities. I dedicate this book to my mentor, Ben Newman, whose unwavering guidance and support have been a constant source of inspiration throughout my journey and who has given me the courage to write this book. Your wisdom, encouragement, and belief in my abilities have fueled my passion and pushed me to reach greater heights.

To my loving family and Olga, who have always been my pillars of strength and compassion, this book is a reflection of the gratitude I feel for your unwavering support. Your constant encouragement, understanding, and belief in me have been instrumental in shaping my dreams and aspirations.

Thank you for being the foundation upon which my creativity thrives, for instilling in me the values of perseverance, and for reminding me of the importance of forgiveness and understanding. This book is a tribute to the extraordinary bond we share and a testament to the immeasurable impact you have had on my life.

May the pages of this book be a small token of my appreciation for all that you have done and continue to do. Last, but certainly not least, to my boy Sir Henry X: You are and always will be the greatest blessing of my life. Without you, I may not have ever been given a second chance.

With deepest love and gratitude, this book is dedicated to you all.

Read This First

Scan the QR Code to Access Some Free Resources

Life, Lies, & Second Chances

Developing Resilience to Overcome Adversity

Robby S. Fakhouri

www.GameChangerPublishing.com

Foreword

I meet thousands of people in the course of my work. All of them are talented, successful, and driven by the desire to want an even better life than they have now. I value every one of those interactions, but due to the nature of my schedule, it's difficult for me to carve out as much time as I'd like to get to know most of them as deeply as I want.

However, once in a great while, a person comes along that is so dynamic and electric that I make it a priority to connect with them regularly after the fact. That is the best way for me to describe my relationship with Robby Fakhouri. We started as casual acquaintances, then he became a coaching client, and now I consider Robby a dear and trusted friend.

As I got to know him, I became even more fascinated by his life story and the obstacles he has overcome. I was thrilled when he first told me he was writing *Life, Lies, & Second Chances: Developing Resilience to Overcome Adversity* because I knew Robby would pour the same vivid passion into this book as he does with all things in his life.

More than that, because I know his story, I know what these pages will reveal. How Robby overcame his struggles can be a blueprint to help you with whatever battles you're fighting in your life.

Robby has approached this book with candor and a fire in his belly. That means you will get a raw, no-holds-barred account of his battles with substance abuse, self-deception, and failure that just about killed him.

But you'll also read about his journey out of the darkness and into the light and Robby's moments of clarity that saved his life. Ultimately, when he took ownership of his actions, this became a story about rebuilding all he had lost through grit and accountability to himself and others he cared about.

The best part of Robby's story is that just like he owned his failures earlier in life, Robby now gets to own the second chance he has given himself.

Some of you will see your life as a reflection of what Robby has gone through. And that's the point.

By relating to the insights and lessons Robby has learned about himself, *Life, Lies, & Second Chances* can become part of your path to the new chapters in your own lives that every one of you deserves.

HUGE praise to Robby for the resilience and discipline required to turn his life around.

More importantly, I admire Robby for having the courage to tell his story.

And I am confident that after you've turned the last page of this book, you will come to the same conclusions as I did.

Ben Newman
USA Today Top 5 Performance Coach
2x Wall Street Journal Bestseller

Table of Contents

Introduction 1

Chapter 1 – All the Feelings, None of the Reasoning 5

Chapter 2 – The Lies that Motivate Our Demise 29

Chapter 3 – The Effect of Masking, Instead of Dealing 43

Chapter 4 – No Purpose, No Future 55

Chapter 5 – A Second Chance 63

Chapter 6 – The Rise of Resilience 77

Chapter 7 – The Haunting Consequences of Our Past 87

Chapter 8 – The Standard of Resilience 103

Conclusion – A Strong Mind 121

Introduction

This isn't a biography. This is a real, raw, firsthand, authentic account of ultimate failure due to self-inflicted behavior, substance abuse, and addiction—so grave, so great—that the idea of life, the simple opportunity to breathe, was no more.

This is not a story about me. It's a story about life, lies, and second chances. The journey to rock bottom is filled with the consequences of our actions, the lies we tell ourselves, and the external pressures that influence our behaviors and decision-making. And therein lies the problem. The simple fact is that when we allow our conduct to be dictated by our feelings, external pressures, or the "what if?" we lose control. We mask, we hide, we avoid.

This story provides insight into how to make changes and find stability, confidence, and strength from within—changes in mind and body that require a level of discipline and consistent effort that will empower you. Beyond making an impact, this is a story of the struggle while you struggle—to tell you that only you can determine if things will be okay. This is a story of accountability. To understand why we are where we are, we must first understand how we got there. The lies that we tell ourselves. The excuses that we make up for our circumstances. Those lies, no matter how slight, can alter our path forward. The question of whether you can persevere is only answered from within. The truth is that, irrespective of whatever tragedy you think you're going through or have gone through, you will always determine the path forward, your conduct, your responses, and, most importantly, your ability to face adversity without allowing your thoughts and your mind to dictate your response.

So often, we are led to believe that one wrong turn and it's all over. But who determines that? I've learned that no matter the adversity, the answer to that question is me—for you, it's you. That is this story. One challenge that, at least for me, I thought I would never be able to overcome. Even after successfully overcoming it six years later, I was still haunted by the consequences of those past failures. The unfortunate, sad, disappointing, and almost cosmic return of that past became the most enlightening time of my life, during which I realized what true resilience and strength require.

The discipline that I built over the years would be faced with the ultimate test, in the most public of ways, and would call into question my goals and future. The doubts and fears that I finally believed I had overcome resurfaced, and the physical pain, stress, and mental suffering I knew so well returned in an almost paralyzing way. But it was in that very moment, and the months and years that followed, that I *chose* to maintain the daily discipline and commitment to my goals, my fitness, and peace of mind. This moment of enlightenment revealed my ultimate strength—my unformidable resilience to preserve because of the second chance at life I was given.

That resilience was built by a daily, consistent, relentless pursuit and commitment to overcoming my past and becoming the best version of myself in mind and body. Resilience is not something you build overnight. It's taken years of focus, dedication, and a commitment to my health, nutrition, and fitness. A daily discipline incorporated into everyday life, including physical activity, talk therapy, and fasting, has given me the tools and strength to persevere. These are the tools you will learn; these are tools that can make a difference in your future, no matter what you face.

In this story, I hope to provide you, or someone you know, with the strength, the example, and, most importantly, the mindset to build the stability you'll need because life is never linear. Life is a rollercoaster, fraught with ups and downs, which requires discipline, resilience, and inner strength to avoid being shaken by external pressures or internal feelings. That's the story.

For the first time in my life, I am writing this book truly openly, without trying to prove something to someone, without the insecurities that guide our conduct and actions, whether consciously or subconsciously. This project will be revealed once completed, and it speaks volumes about growth.

If there is one thing you should take away even before knowing this story, it is that whatever you do in your life, you have to do it for yourself.

CHAPTER 1

All the Feelings, None of the Reasoning

French philosopher René Descartes famously said, "I think, therefore I am." A philosophy I've always lived and been inspired by. "I think, therefore I am." I will be what I say I will be. How powerful is that philosophy? It's a question of the mind. But the mind can be dangerous. It can inflict severe pain without discipline and acknowledgment of struggle and difficulties, external pressures, internal failures, and insecurities. But for me, "I think, therefore I am" took control of me—my feelings, my mind, my thoughts, that is. I allowed it to ruin me. To destroy all of me and whatever it was I thought I was supposed to be.

By the very simple effect of my mind and my feelings—at a time of colossal, cataclysmic failure, all at once in my face, with nothing to do but... try, just try—to save, protect, and maybe, just maybe, give back for what was always given. For me, "I think, therefore I am" drove me to do things, to become someone, to become so isolated that the man I know I am, the one I have always thought I would become, was an impossibility. So, I have to take you back. Not too far, but just enough to know.

My childhood, my family background, and my upbringing are where we begin. You see, we are all a product of our environment. I am a first-generation Jordanian American who grew up witnessing parents who came from absolutely nothing. A father who fled a country as a Christian refugee to the United States to make an opportunity for himself. My father, one of 10, couldn't even afford to have his entire family come to this country. In the late 1970s, six of my father's seven brothers came to Chicago, Illinois, while the rest of his family stayed in Jordan. In his journey to obtaining the American Dream, his first line of work was taking roses from the back of a dumpster outside of a funeral home and selling them on the street in the north side of Chicago. My mother, born in southwest Detroit, was one of seven children who grew up with little to no means. My maternal grandfather, whom I never had the benefit of knowing, was a union worker as a mechanic at a trucking company, struggling to give my mother and her siblings a chance at the American dream.

For me, I never knew that life. What I did know was growth, bearing witness to my mother and father's effort—the relentless, consistent, persistent work ethic they displayed. My two sisters, Deala and Crystal, and I saw it firsthand day after day because they had no choice but to bring us to work with them. In the most dangerous Chicago neighborhoods, as kids, every day, my sisters and I were there—no matter the hour, no matter the day (so long as we were not in school)—we were with them. We not only witnessed but were victims of crimes that I've never shared. I've seen my mom physically fight off patrons who attempted to rob our stores, M-80s thrown just feet away from my sisters and me, and, in the 5th grade, my sister Crystal and I were robbed at gunpoint.

Even so, my parents wanted us to know what real work was. Whether it was restaurants, liquor stores, convenience stores—I mean, you name it, they tackled it. When prepaid cell phone service was a thing, they had more than ten cell phone stores scattered throughout the Chicagoland area, and we worked at all of them. They taught us that you have to scrub the toilet before taking a shit in it; it was as simple as that. My parents showed us what real work was, but the pride in their work was not for them—it was for us, especially me. I was their baby boy, the only son. There were over 1,500 bus stops around the City of Chicago that had "Robby's Communication" stamped on every bench. That was their glory.

My parents built a fortune for themselves, and my two sisters and I were the beneficiaries of it, to a fault. They had never known what it was like to have any sort of wealth. But their dedication, their love, and their adoration for their kids came before reason. They didn't put their business and themselves first; they sacrificed their kids' happiness to their detriment, to their financial failure.

My parents gave us everything, and I literally mean everything. It is an embarrassing account when looking back at it now, but an example of that sacrificial love began when I was 15 years old in a small suburb outside of Chicago called Bloomingdale. My childhood friends and our parents were all very close and regularly visited a local sushi restaurant called Abashiri. There was always a group of us and our parents, but sometimes one of the friends and their parents couldn't make it. But not this one time. Everyone was there this time—no one was missing except my dad. I didn't realize my parents had arranged it until I got a call from my dad to come outside. And there it was, at 15, my learner's permit car—a brand new Chevrolet Tahoe with a big bow and 22-inch rims. This was a time when rims were a thing, I'm talking *Pimp My Ride* from the MTV days. As we all walked outside in celebration, I stood completely still, and everyone awaited my response.

And oh, did I respond! In front of everyone, like a complete asshole: "Eww, you bought me a Chevy!" Everyone laughed, even my parents, but I knew it broke them. So what did they do? They traded in that brand-new truck for a $90,000 BMW 650i. Ridiculous, looking back on it. Absurd.

But that's who they were. That's who they are. That's what they wanted to give. They didn't even want us to know what it was like. They wanted to give us the world and everything in it. They never wanted their kids to experience a life of financial difficulty.

And I will say that despite what may be perceived as irresponsibility, lack of appreciation, and maybe just being a spoiled little teenager, for me, it was motivation. It is what told me, pushed me to say, "I will be the best at what I choose to pursue." The life they provided motivated me to achieve greatness. And as a child, I would prove greatness through academic excellence in high school, college, and law school.

In fact, every time I excelled, I was rewarded. After completing high school in three and a half years and being accepted into Loyola University of Chicago on a scholarship, I was rewarded. At 17, my parents bought me a matte black $150,000 Mercedes-Benz G-Wagon G55 AMG and a million-dollar condo in downtown Chicago. There I was, living on my own in the only building east of Lakeshore Drive, Chicago's infamous Lake Point Tower, in a condo with a view that, thinking back on it now, I have never seen matched in the city to this day.

It motivated me. It drove me. It told me that if this is where I'm starting and looking at where my parents are, I have no choice but to succeed. But inside of me, there was this fear, this unrelenting fear brewing deeper and deeper. Will I achieve that success professionally like I did academically? I became so burdened with all that privilege—strange, I know, but true.

Fast forward to December 2013, and, of course, I couldn't finish law school the way others did—taking my time, that is. To me, education and getting my degree were the only things standing in the way of starting my future. Education was simply a burden that needed to be completed before I could set out on my own and make something of myself. I had to do it as quickly as possible, without interruption. So I went year-round, college and law school—college in three years, law school in two and a half. But there was something else motivating me inside.

Truthfully, having been born on May 7th, I knew that if I completed law school in two and a half years and took the February bar exam, I could become one of the youngest attorneys in Illinois, licensed at 23 years old. I had to do that. I needed to accomplish that. Not so much for me, but to say it to others. Sure, I am proud of it. Part of me did it for me, but looking back on it, I question if that is what best served me. The point here is to always do what best serves you.

So, it was time to get a job. I interviewed at one of Illinois' largest personal injury law firms, right on Wacker Drive and State Street in the heart of downtown Chicago, right off the river. I met with the owner of the firm, and I remember he looked at my wrist and said, "Where did you get that watch?"

I was like, "Huh?"

I didn't even realize the lack of appreciation. I was wearing a $50,000 Audemars Piguet, one of many, frankly. Every year, I was given a watch from my dad. It was his way of saying, "Keep going." I think that led to something my boss-to-be told me at the end of that interview. I recall him sharing a story that his grandfather had told him: "If you can put your toe in the doorway, you should, and then wait for the opportunity for the door to open before stepping in."

I didn't get an answer if I got the job at that time. I received an email later that evening and was offered a position as a law clerk. I was insulted. But I remembered what he said. I took it as a challenge and knew my work ethic would prove me worthy. I took the job. Three months later, I was promoted to attorney, and my journey began.

But let's fast forward to the day it all came down. Oh, did it come down. Crashing, harder, faster, scarier than I could have ever imagined.

The phone rings in my office, and I receive a call from reception, saying, "The sheriff's here."

I replied, "What? Why would the sheriff be here on one of my cases? If they needed to serve something, they would serve the individual—not the attorney." I thought I was teaching the receptionist something, and my annoying young lawyer's ego came out.

She responded, "I think you should come to the front."

And, so I went. But, it was not about a case I was working on. They were not looking for a client of mine. I was the one they were looking for. I was the one being sued. I was served with an eviction. It's important to say my parents were still paying for everything even though I had a job. The only thing I wouldn't let them pay for was my law school. That was something I had to own because, with everything that was given, the burden of what was given always consumed me—a burden from them that I didn't want to say they gave me. This was something I had to give myself—my degree. I didn't want anyone to own that but me, so I took out student loans.

But back to the day it all came crashing down. I looked at the papers, and they said *"eviction"* and listed me as one of the defendants because I was technically just a tenant. My father owned the property.

I went back to my office and closed the door. I was so confused, so angry, and enraged that something was going on with my family, especially legally, without me knowing. I was a lawyer; how could they not let me know? But then again, my parents were unwilling to let their kids know of their struggle. That's who they were. But this time, they had no choice—they were exposed.

So I called my father and asked, "What the hell is going on?!"

"What do you mean you have it taken care of?!"

"Don't worry about it?!"

In my head, now was my time. It was my time to give them back everything they've given me. That's what I thought. That's what I owed them.

That year, however, I only earned a $50,000 salary as an attorney. The good thing was the work ethic I always had allowed me to sign 37 personal injury cases. If you know anything about personal injury law, that's a really big deal. For my firm, it was the most that any lawyer had signed in a single year.

So I went to the boss that day and said, "I need to make more money. I have to take care of my parents." I didn't know what the heck I was saying or doing at that time. In fact, I completely lacked the ability, nor did I appreciate, the financial responsibility that I bestowed upon myself. I never was responsible for paying for things on my own. I never knew what it was like to be responsible for bills on a monthly basis—at least, recurring ones. While working at that firm, my entire salary was sent to the financial aid department to pay down my student loans. I don't know if my boss didn't believe me, but he was very honest in his response. He said, "One day, I think you will want a chair like mine, and my son is here, and I just can't give you that raise."

Coming from a Mediterranean background (he was an Italian-American), I understood that love for family. I actually appreciated his forwardness. I respected it and understood why he said what he said. Still, I just wanted to work at an established company instead of building my own brick-and-mortar. But that wasn't an option.

So I told myself, wearing that metaphorical superhero cape, that it was time to start saving. The time for action was now. In that building, there were 39 or 40 floors at One East Wacker Drive. On that particular day, I went down every single floor until I discovered an office on the 23rd floor. It belonged to another personal injury attorney who occupied half a floor and had his own firm. There was a storage area on the back left side, no door, just an open space with furniture, chairs, desks, and boxes—it was quite a mess. When I look back at the photo of that space, I can't help but laugh now.

The owner of the firm said, "You can have that. I'll remove everything."

I said, "Okay, but could I build a wall and put up a door?"

"Sure," he said, "but you've got to pay for it."

Well, I didn't have any money, and neither did my parents. I mean, I had some, but nowhere near enough.

So I called the financial aid department for student loans and said, "I paid $23,000 this year, and you guys never gave me the option of an income-based repayment plan." I begged for weeks for them to send me my money back because I needed it, and they did. I was shocked, but that $23,000 gave me what I needed. I built a wall, put up a door, and spent a little extra so the door could have a glass with the law firm's logo, making me feel like this was my space. This was my opportunity to build a future.

But the problem was much bigger than that. It wasn't just about starting a law firm without enough experience and, frankly, not knowing my ass from my head. It was now trying to save a portfolio of $25 million in real estate and realizing the extent of what happened to my parents.

You see, I had to become the lawyer I knew I wanted to be. I had to investigate every single aspect of how the fuck this situation had occurred. Here's what I learned: There was a bank in Chicago that my father and his brothers had always used. In commercial real estate, there are usually two accounts—one that operates the commercial business and another that is an escrow account to ensure taxes are paid. So when there are business loans on those commercial properties, the taxes are never an issue and are always paid.

Well, my dad received notice of a tax sale on his biggest property, where he owed, I believe, three million dollars, and he would lose the property if it wasn't paid. His fury led him to that bank, refusing to pay his commercial notes until those taxes were paid. The money was in escrow, and the taxes should have been paid. Instead of ensuring he kept his loans in good standing, he told the bank owner to "fuck off" and that he wouldn't pay his commercial notes until the bank paid the taxes from the money that should have been in escrow.

What my father didn't know was that the bank was under investigation by the FDIC and just months away from being shut down.

When they finally took the bank down, the commercial notes were in default. The taxes still didn't get paid. But now, the noteholder had changed. The bank went up for auction. And in those situations, at auction, the FDIC splits the good notes from the bad notes. The bad notes are for the vultures, the powerhouses—ones that, frankly, I respect, having dealt with them at least, simply for their business acumen. Now, he wasn't just dealing with that banker he'd known for years; he was dealing with an entity out of Texas that he didn't know. A strength in capital and bankroll that would push him out simply because of the cash flow—the positive operating income.

I investigated it all. I looked into every document, every record. And there it was—forged signatures. All of our family's properties, our homes, my condo, other commercial properties—all of it was cross-collateralized. Which means if one falls, they all fall. I was livid. I remember vividly what I turned that once beautiful apartment into. It was like an episode of *Hoarders*. My entire condominium was covered—you couldn't see a tile if you tried. Boxes, paperwork, documentation on their entire commercial portfolio dating back five, ten years, whenever the origination of the purchase happened, I went through it. I separated it. All of this at the same time I was trying to start a law practice.

What I wasn't focusing on and wasn't realizing was the tragedy, failure, and lack of finances and the responsibility of trying to save everything overwhelmed me. Truly, at least in terms of my intentions, the desire to save because I had been so blessed was simply more than one person at 25 years old could handle.

Sadly, it required more than just me. But it was just me. I knew I needed help. I needed more hours in the day, which takes us to the worst day of them all—the final day before leaving the firm. There was another attorney in that office whom I had known and worked well with. He was 5 or 7 years older than I, but someone I had graduated with. He knew what was going on. I shared what I was trying to do to save my family's real estate and open the new firm. I recall him saying something along the lines of, "I don't know how the heck you're going to do all this, but I know a doctor."

Those words, that fucking information. I wish I would have never known.

He continued and said, there's a doctor on Michigan Avenue that I go to at 900 North Michigan Avenue, and she'll prescribe you anything you need. If you've been to Chicago, that address is the crème de la crème. It's Oak Street and Michigan Avenue—the Magnificent Mile. The Gold Coast is what they call it, with the fanciest stores. The doctor was in that building. He said, "She'll give you what you need (Adderall, that is). Just tell her you took Adderall in high school but stopped, and now you have so much to do that it's hard to focus. She'll give it to you. It will take five minutes. That's all you have to say, trust me." I wish I hadn't.

I had never taken prescription medication before. I never used it in school, took it, or was prescribed it in high school, law school, or even after. I didn't need that. It was my effort that had gotten me where I was all along. But in my mind, of course, I needed something. I mean, we've all seen the movie *Limitless*, right? That's what I thought of. That's what will do the trick.

He was so right. I went in, and in maybe less than five minutes, I got the prescription. The first of many. That started around February 2016 when I opened my firm. But what about saving the family business? I had to hire lawyers. I had to pay those lawyers a retainer fee. They said, "We can save this. We see your point. We see the case."

For me, it allowed me to put saving those properties, at least on a legal side, in the hands of a professional. I understood the facts. I laid it out. It was organized. I just needed them to be lawyers—I didn't practice commercial litigation. I had a personal injury firm to build. I needed to make money to support my family, to support myself, to run my business, right?

What I wasn't focusing on, what I left completely in the dark was myself, what I was going through, my struggle. And slowly, the effect of "I think therefore I am," my feelings and my concerns overwhelmed me. I couldn't sleep. I kept taking more Adderall and running out of Adderall. I needed more time. How can I get this all done? I mean, I literally started a firm without any help or knowledge two years in. I didn't even know how to file paperwork to start a business, let alone register a law firm and do the proper procedures. And no one was there to help. Not because I didn't want them to, but because every mentor, everyone around me, every true professional, with all due respect to them, said, "Don't do this. It is not your problem. You'll be okay. You have to find another firm. You can't take this on."

But they didn't understand my family. Maybe it was our culture. Maybe they didn't understand me, the burden I've always felt for what I've always been given. But those thoughts, *You're going to fail, it's too soon.* That never left the back of my mind. I had to give it my all. I had to save my family, even if it meant losing myself in the process.

The story of where my parents originated from, coming from humble beginnings, drove me. It drove me in the absolute wrong direction, and I continued into the abyss of complete and utter failure.

The Adderall was no longer "giving me more time," I became a hamster on a wheel. The pill that was supposed to give me focus was now the only thing I focused on. My body started to deteriorate. I was in pain from all of the amphetamine. On some, if not most, days, I would take more than 300 milligrams of Adderall. I was taking way too much. That doctor who gave the prescription so easily, well, she also increased the dosage just as easily. And, now, those appointments that were a minute or two became longer. I set out with a goal. I needed a pill to fix every problem. I had to find something to help me sleep. I needed something for the pain. I needed more Adderall. I was running out of my monthly prescription in a week., maybe two. The stress became worse. I needed to escape my reality. That's how it all begins—addiction, that is. A substance that allows you to escape your reality. It's the most dangerous aspect of any addiction.

At this point, the thought of failing was all-consuming, and I expressed that to the doctor, not for actual psychiatric purposes but for more medication. And oh, did the doctor give! Samples of different medications, stocked in her office, were passed to me like candy to a trick-or-treater on Halloween. "Try this. Maybe this will work," she'd say. I took whatever she would give, whatever I could, to escape my reality.

Two years in (in 2018), everything I was trying to save was slipping away, and nothing was coming to fruition. The law firm was so difficult to manage. I wasn't even paying attention. All I was concerned with at that point was another pill. It was the only way to get out of my fearful head. The only way I could continue to lie to myself about what was really going on.

The problem was the fear of what would happen; the lies I was telling myself began to control my conduct.

And there it is— the dangerous effect of "I think, therefore, I am."

This is the power of thought, and you must be careful of your thoughts because they become your words. Your words become your actions, and your actions lead to consequences—consequences that can shape your character and alter your destiny.

So, let's fast forward because we have to get to the point. The point where the idea of life was something I no longer wanted. The insecurities I displayed were a facade for the internal battle I was fighting. For me, there was no turning back. It was all over. The eviction happened. I was in my car, going from one place to another, sometimes sleeping in the car. There was no home. I became so angry. I hated everything about my parents because the more I learned, the more I realized that they just sacrificed everything for us. And I was so mad.

How could they be so stupid? Where did they save? How did they not save? These questions led me to think—*it's their fault.* My failures were not mine, but theirs. I began to make excuses. I continued to lie.

I separated myself from everyone and anyone that I knew. It wasn't just because of the weight of everything that was destroying me. It's because I didn't want anyone to know. There was a comfort attached to taking prescription medication. The fact that the substance I used to escape my reality was prescription medication made it okay—like I didn't have a problem. Going to Walgreens or any pharmacy and seeing a doctor meant I wasn't a drug addict, at least in my own mind; it was medication, it was prescribed. Again, it was a lie. The truth was I was an addict, no matter how I tried to spin it.

In the year before February 2018, my mom was working for me at the law office because I couldn't afford to pay anyone, and my addiction was becoming too obvious. I was recognizing my addiction. I didn't have any money, at least not enough to keep things going or to pay an employee, but I had my mom working for me at the firm. I mean, my mom didn't even know what a deposition was. Every time a client called, she would say I was in a deposition, but in reality, I was just in the back office, accomplishing nothing, merely spinning like a hamster on a wheel due to taking excessive Adderall just to wake up and get out of bed.

I told myself in February of 2018 that I should let my mom go. But she was just trying to be a supportive mother; more importantly, she wanted to ensure her son was okay. When I wouldn't show up to the office, she'd come to my house and see me curled up, asking, "Why are you in so much pain?" She knew. She definitely knew. But she felt to blame. I think she felt responsible, and it made her scared. She just wanted to be there to make sure nothing happened. However, the office couldn't continue like that, so to take control, my mom had to leave.

I wanted to save my law firm while at the same time not wanting to be exposed at the same time. It was a Friday. I remember vividly that I told my mom she couldn't work for me anymore to force me to find someone to help. The following Monday morning I found my savior in the elevator. The one person who would be the reason I might succeed—Olga Ramos. The world works in mysterious ways, and it could not have been better timing.

And here's something you should know. Olga came from the old law firm that I worked at. That Monday in the elevator was the first time I had seen her since I had left two years before. Olga looked at me and said, "How are you doing?"

Of course, I lied and said, "I'm doing great. How are you?"

She said, "I am doing good. How is the firm?"

The only truth that came out of my mouth at that time was that I was looking to hire an assistant, but I said it as if the firm was succeeding. I knew I needed someone with skill, and she didn't just have the skill—she was a beast. The master of all masters in handling cases, being organized, and getting the job done. If she worked for me, in my mind, there was no way I could fail. She would get me out of this awful hole. The idea of her working for me was as if God had just dropped this blessing; I didn't even think it was an option that I couldn't afford to pay her. To make a long story short, she said she was looking for a job and would bring down her resume.

I said, "What? Your resume? You are hired now." Well, that day, she sent me a printed-out resume because she is so professional. I looked at her honestly, for the first time, and said that I couldn't pay her what she had been making at the other firm. I knew she wasn't being paid enough, which is a big problem in the personal injury industry. But I made her promises. I told her it would take time, but I promised it would be worth it if we did it together. She trusted me. She never should have, but she did because she saw how hard I worked in my first two years out of law school. She said okay.

But my addiction, even with the responsibility just placed on me, having one of the best assistants I could ever ask for—someone with a family, three kids, a husband, and who traveled on a train 50 minutes in the treacherous cold—I didn't even recognize that. My addiction didn't allow me to. I was lying to her as much as I was lying to myself. How fucking selfish—how fucking reckless.

But that's what addiction does. Addiction does not discriminate in its harm. It affects the addict and everyone around them. And, even with Olga working for me now, my addiction was out of control. I started getting flagged. I couldn't go to some pharmacies because I was trying to refill too early. I kept calling the doctor, saying I lost my medication just to get a refill. It became a problem. I started buying off the street. My body pain, my mental suffering, all of it was just something I didn't want to deal with. I was lying to myself—about my business, about how bad everything was. I was even lying when I said I wasn't responsible for destroying everything.

At the same time, these medications caused me to lose the clarity required to run my business. I was writing checks to pay for costs on client case files without keeping things separate, as I was required to by my license and ethically obligated to do so. I commingled everything just to get by. That was it; I reached my breaking point on July 11, 2018.

I thought, *I can't fix this. I can't fix this.* The law firm was fucked. I was fucked. I had no relationship with friends, my sisters, or family. At this point, I was on nine different medications. That's the truth. Anti-suicide, Lorazepam, Gabapentin, Prozac, Adderall, Xanax, the dosages, Jesus Christ, I didn't know how my heart didn't stop. At the time of my overdose, I was prescribed 120 30-milligram pills of Adderall, another prescription for 20 milligrams, and an additional 30 pills of 10 milligrams every month. Of course, I had to inform the doctor that my body had developed this tolerance. As for Xanax, I received 90 2-milligram bars with each prescription. This doesn't include what I would buy off the street. I could not tell you how much I was buying as I sit here today, but I know it was a lot.

The problem was I'd run out of my prescriptions in a week, maybe two at most. I turned to the street to purchase these prescriptions to avoid running out of supply before my next refill was set to fill. It was disgusting. How could I even be functioning? I don't even really remember that whole time. I mean, imagine, with all the medication, it was a blur. That's not to make excuses. I own everything. All of who I am, as you'll hear and see. But those pharmacies, the street guys, I couldn't get them right away. I was finally tired of being so consumed by the supply, running out of pills, and finding a way to get more.

So that day in the summer of 2018, I told Olga I'd be right back, got in a taxi, and found a pharmacy far over on the south side of Chicago that could fill my prescription. I wasn't in their system. I would not be flagged. I could get my refill. And in the taxi, I said to myself, *Oh my God, how did you get here? You had so much promise. You were going to be someone great.* Well, I had enough. I was over it—life that was. I wanted out. I wanted to end my life.

If there is anything I remember during this time, it is this: I am in the back of the taxi alone. The pill bottles were in a white package. I ripped the top off and grabbed the bottle of Xanax. I poured them into my palm, maybe 5 or 6, 2 mg bars. I took all of them. What a coward I was, trying to take the easy way out.

After that, I have no idea what happened next. The only thing I remember is waking up in the Emergency Room at Northwestern Hospital. Olga saved me.

After I didn't return to the office, Olga got worried and had the building where I was living conduct a wellness check. They found me on the floor, with my head busted open, passed out, and lifeless. I had overdosed and hit my head on the edge of the dresser but failed in my attempt to take my own life.

When I came to, I saw at the edge of my hospital bed my father, who I had stopped talking to for at least a year and a half at this point, and a friend from high school's mother, Felicia, whose son had passed from a heroin overdose just a year or two into my college years. I was mortified. I was exposed. Worst of all, I failed at taking my own life, and now my addiction couldn't be hidden anymore. I couldn't lie about it anymore.

I didn't respond with gratitude and appreciation. I said, "That's not fucking me. I'm not a heroin addict." I was lying to myself. An addict is an addict. It's not dealing. It doesn't matter what the choice is to escape reality. It could be alcohol or a prescription medication; frankly, it could be any drug. That is because addiction is driven by your mind. The substance that you choose just allows you to escape. It allows you to avoid. It separates you from reality. That's something I learned.

But in the hospital that day, I knew at 28 years old that they couldn't force me to do a thing. And I ripped out the IVs and ran out of that hospital. I took off. I left the hospital and flew out of town with my boy.

I haven't even talked about my boy. You've got to know about him—an English Bulldog named Sir Henry that I got when I opened my firm. He's my lifesaver, and I truly believe he saved my life. Just for a laugh, I'll tell you a story about Christmas in 2017, months before I hired Olga. That Christmas, I was completely alone. I didn't have a place to live, and I didn't know where I was going to go. So, I thought I'd treat myself and stay at a hotel for Christmas Eve, all by myself.

Henry was still a puppy. He was born in July. I was still working on training him. That Christmas morning was like a harbinger of what was to come. I woke up in the bed with shit all around me. Christmas morning, I woke up with dog shit all around the bed. It was literally in my face. I just looked at my life and said, "Everything is full of shit and here it is. Merry fucking Christmas."

Anyway, I took Henry, and we flew to New York. I didn't answer anyone's calls, but I got one call I knew I had to answer. It was Olga. She said she was out. She said I quit. How could I let her leave a place that gave her so much stability? I remember exactly where I was when I got the call. I was near Hell's Kitchen in New York. I was standing by an old telephone, you know, those telephones that used to be out on the street, where people could make collect calls. I just fell to the ground, and I started crying. I knew that was it. I had to change. I begged her to stay, but she said no. There was nothing I could say. I was exposed. I let her down beyond measure. My selfishness just put her entire family at risk. I didn't deserve her.

Then, my parents called. They said, "Come home, it will be okay. We will fix this together." I knew I needed help. I knew now more than ever that I had lost myself to my addiction. My family was great, so I listened and returned home. Their compassion and convincing my assistant to stay. They did all of that for me. That's who they were. But I had to go to rehab. I mean, that's what I needed.

So there I was at the airport back in Chicago, and I knew it was time to change. I had no other choice—my parents were determined to help me. Felicia, my friend's mom, who was at the edge of my hospital bed, returned to help my parents find a rehabilitation treatment center. It was not a fancy, luxury rehab center in Malibu like you see on the commercials. No, I went to a place in Rockford, Illinois, called Rosecrance, a place I now proudly sit on the committee of.

My addiction, my attempt to take my own life, is not just about substance abuse for me. It's not just about sharing a story of overcoming addiction but also about overcoming a suicide attempt.

It's to give somebody else the light that I never had. If I had that light, oh, I wish I had that light. Well, it was finally being given to me. But it didn't take me once or twice to be driven all the way to Rockford from where I grew up. I couldn't find the courage to go inside. And the pills, by the way, even though I was going to go to rehab, I hid them before I left New York. I put them in the lining of the suitcase and emptied the prescription bottles so all the pills would just sit in the interior lining of the suitcase. I knew my parents would check my bags. They would want to make sure; any loving parent would.

That's how far my addiction had gone. Even when I accepted what it truly was, I couldn't do without a pill. I didn't know how to get up or go to bed, none of that without this pill, but many pills. On the second attempt, I was crying and said, "I can't go in," and stayed outside. My father went back inside and told them, "He's just not ready."

However, I was trying to trick my dad. I ran back to the car to open the lining of the suitcase that was still in the trunk. It had never left the trunk of his car. But he caught me. He looked at me and said, "You see? Habibi, you have a problem." "Habibi" is an Arabic term for "my love."

Still, in the face of disgust, he showed compassion. I never thought that before. The pills were gone. He threw them all away, ripped apart the luggage, and made me watch him throw them all out one by one. He was angry, but he knew it wasn't his son. That wasn't me. Addiction, abuse—I taught that man that it's true. It's real. It's a disease. I learned about substance abuse, what it does to a person, how it alters their mind, their sense of reality, and their ability to think clearly and act. Without help, you can't overcome it because you're lost.

So I went the next day. I was admitted. I felt like I was going to jail, stripped naked, completely checked, given a uniform, and all my clothes were placed in a plastic bag, only to be put in a small room with two wooden beds and a shared bathroom. I was with an older gentleman who told me this was his third time there; he was a heroin addict. Probably in his 40s, but he looked 60. I was terrified. How did I get here?

And then I remembered. "I think, therefore I am." I did it. Only me. My first day there, I had to get in line to take some medication because of the amount of Xanax that was in my system. If I didn't take whatever pill the rehab center gave me, I would have a seizure. That's what they told me. You only got one or two calls a day, if I remember.

On the second day, I called my parents in complete and utter fear. Despite being 28 years old, I felt like a child, begging and yearning for my parents to save me. I told them I'd move back home, promising to stay sober, with them watching me 24/7. The rehab center advised against it because I was actually detoxing, and that was terrible. I was constantly throwing up. When I walked into that rehab facility, I was maybe 160 pounds wet, 5'10", just skin and bones. All those prescriptions and drugs had deteriorated my body. And it didn't end once my parents agreed that I could leave the rehab center and move back in with them, with them watching over me. I didn't realize I'd continue to detox until one night (I think it was the first or second) when I found myself dry-heaving over the toilet on the first floor of my parents' home. My dad came because he heard me, put a cold towel over my neck, rubbed my back, and said, "Baba, it's going to be okay," meaning, "Son, it is going to be okay."

That statement alone convinced me that I had to get out of this. I had to let it out, literally, physically, emotionally, entirely. The idea of being a complete and utter failure wasn't an option. This was not who I am. I was going to make a change. I promised myself I'd do so slowly. I promised myself I would take it one step at a time.

There it is. Manifestation is real. I had to take back control. I had to end the lies.

So ask yourself, *Who is responsible for where you are? Who is responsible for the circumstances you are in today? Are your thoughts leading your actions? Are your feelings controlling and determining your outcome and your conduct?*

These are things that I had to consider. I had to stop lying to myself. I had to take accountability. I was just given a second chance at life.

These are things that you must consider. The way you think a circumstance will result will manifest into reality. Our mind, consciously and subconsciously, will control our responses, our conduct, and our actions.

So before we move on, ask yourself, *How do you think of a problem? Are you focused on the negative outcome? Are you focused on what others think of you and your decisions? Is that judgment affecting your actions? Is it controlling your decision-making?* Most of all, *Are you lying to yourself about why you are? What is it that is causing your current circumstance?* All of that will determine your future. You are the only one responsible for what tomorrow will bring.

CHAPTER 2

The Lies that Motivate Our Demise

Lies. Oh, the lies that we tell ourselves. But why? Why do we lie? What is it that motivates our demise? To take control and truly give yourself a second chance at life, you must first understand what motivates your demise. This is where I began. I had to understand the lies—the reason why I hit rock bottom. It was in those weeks and months that followed my overdose that I had to come to terms with my circumstances. The compounded chaos that I created. I had to take accountability.

The lies that we tell ourselves and others, as well as the motivations behind those lies, may not matter as much as the lie itself. Why? Because the temporary avoidance created by the lie has consequences far beyond momentary relief.

Oh, and how I lied. I lied to myself, and I lied to everyone. All because I didn't want to deal with it. I didn't want to own my addiction; I didn't want to recognize the insecurities of what I was going through. I needed to deny it. I needed to avoid it. I lied to escape my reality, but all I was actually doing was making matters far worse than they needed to be.

I needed to prove myself, not for my sake, but for others. It didn't matter whether I was acting out in an effort to maintain the image of what was lost because, in the end, I knew the simple choice not to deal with my reality was the problem. That was the lie. That was the easy way out.

My choice in trying to take my own life led to me being completely exposed. I couldn't lie anymore. Not to myself, not to my family, not to my friends, certainly not to my business, nor clients. I had to fix it all. But first, I had to understand the lies. I had to know why I was there. How did I get there? And I realized that those lies are what motivated my demise.

The first of those lies begins with the self—physically and mentally. I began taking Adderall in the hopes that it would give me more time, more focus, and more energy to take care of what was before me.

I doubted what I was physically capable of doing, but the body is far more capable than we can ever imagine—both in its ability to perform and recover. The simple truth is that life, truth in and of itself, is a battle of perceptions, even our own perceptions, the ones we fail to acknowledge, treat, cure, or address. These are our own struggles, problems within ourselves, within our control, that hinder our growth.

We may not realize that some of our actions, if not most of our actions, are attempts to prove something to ourselves or to someone else. The reality was I was never serving myself. In fact, I doubted myself entirely. That's where the problem began. That's where medication became my cover, my choice. I had to dig deep following my overdose, following an attempt to take my own life, to truly understand how I got there. And that's such an important part of overcoming any difficulty or adversity in our lives because we have to recognize and address the things, the issues, the concerns, whether internal or external, that are affecting our actions.

Lies are the basis of denial. They become the excuse not to take responsibility and action for what is happening. This, in turn, motivates a course of action that will cause us to fail. The fears and doubts we create motivate our demise. They become the cover for dealing with our reality. Worse, the lies we tell ourselves bring to fruition the outcome we fear, the outcome that prevents us from obtaining our goals.

It is far easier to lie to ourselves than to actually deal with reality, or so I thought. This was the biggest lie of them all: the lie that causes doubts in our own abilities and hinders our efforts to take control and action. When we lie about our own capabilities, our capacity to endure is when we deprive ourselves of our actual capabilities. We deprive ourselves of the truth of our power.

The reality is that lies motivate our demise because they create a false foundation or understanding of a situation. We are blinded by the lies that we tell ourselves. When we believe in a lie, we may base our actions and decisions on inaccurate information. I know I did. This can lead to poor choices, misunderstandings, and certainly negative consequences.

Lies begin to erode the trust we have with those around us and damage relationships that are important to our growth and development. This compounded chaos makes it harder to work effectively with individuals or groups. Ultimately, the truth tends to prevail, and the lies unravel, often resulting in the realization of the harmful effects they have caused.

The beginning of my abuse of prescription medication was only made worse when the side effects of overuse consumed me. The physical pain, the inability to sleep, the lack of focus, the restlessness, and muscle pain became more damaging as time went on. The side effects, including the loss of clarity, hallucinations, and outright delusions, destroyed any ability for me to achieve the goals I had set out for myself. I had to come to terms with my physical state and the instability I had created to build a foundation to persevere. This was my first step.

I put aside this endless need to focus on how someone perceived me and what I wanted to project. These were temporary feelings and concerns that had nothing to do with any goal I wanted to achieve. If I was not serving myself and becoming my best self, there was no way I could give the best version of myself to anyone—not to family, friends, or clients.

The most important thing that we can do for ourselves is build the discipline that makes us stronger, more stable, more resilient. But you can't travel down a new path if you don't understand how you got there in the first place. You must unravel the lies. This is when the battle of self became the most important part of my journey to overcoming this issue in addressing my mental health.

Anyone who has ever dealt with substance abuse or knows someone with substance abuse issues knows this is a disease. It's a mental health issue. An issue that cannot go unaddressed. It must be treated.

I now know, even as I write this book and in the lessons I'm learning while doing this here now, that deep within me, despite the confidence I may project and indeed possess, there are many insecurities that I've allowed to control my behavior and dictate the way I make decisions. Some of these decisions were definitely to my detriment and would never allow me to become physically capable or to repair. Without self-acknowledgment, we end up with self-defeat.

Lies deprive us of control because they create a false perception of reality. When someone lies to us, they manipulate the information we receive, making it difficult for us to make informed decisions or take appropriate actions. The same holds true when we lie to ourselves. We lose control over our own lives when our understanding of a situation is distorted by lies.

Lies can erode trust, which is crucial for healthy relationships and effective communication. When trust is broken, we begin to feel uncertain and hesitant, losing our sense of control over the dynamics of a relationship or situation. Lies can lead to further lies or cover-ups, creating a web of deceit that becomes increasingly difficult to maintain, making almost certain complete and utter failure. This can cause anxiety, stress, and a constant fear of being exposed, further diminishing our sense of control over our own lives.

The reality is that lies have the power to disrupt the truth, manipulate perceptions, weaken trust, and cause confusion. They ultimately strip us of the control we need to make well-informed decisions and navigate our lives effectively.

Lies can cause internal conflicts that undermine our self-confidence. When we lie, we may constantly worry about being exposed or face guilt and anxiety over that which we deny. This can lead to a sense of powerlessness and lack of control over our own actions and decisions.

Lies can have ripple effects that impact our overall sense of power and control. If a lie goes unchecked, we further our demise. When the lie is uncovered, it often results in the need to deal with the consequences, such as damaged relationships, legal issues, or reputational harm. Handling these repercussions can be draining, and the negative impact can further erode our ability to maintain power and control over our own lives. But to deny ourselves the opportunity to repair, we deny our own existence.

On the other hand, embracing honesty and integrity can empower us. Being truthful with yourself allows you to build trust and confidence from within. That trust and confidence will naturally build with those around you, foster healthier relationships, and increase our influence to positively affect the outcomes we desire. It also gives us a sense of self-assurance and a firm foundation to navigate life's challenges with resilience and authenticity.

To lie is to undermine our power and control by damaging trust, creating internal conflicts, and resulting in negative consequences.

When we are only concerned with projecting an outward image and denying our own reality, as if it serves us or furthers our goals in life, we ultimately fail. We lie to ourselves. Understanding these aspects can be challenging. It's difficult to comprehend what motivates us to make wrong decisions that negatively impact our lives due to denial.

My problems became clear to me when I made the choice to cut everyone out of my life. My use, overuse, and severe mental health issues, including suicidal ideation, severe depression, and anxiety, prevented me from speaking to those I needed most. I will never hide what I am going through because those who truly love you and care about your future and growth will always be there to inspire, guide, and care about your health and well-being. I know that now, but I did not know that then. I understand that my relationship with myself sets the tone for every other relationship I have.

My addiction denied me that ability. More importantly, it denied me the responsibilities I had. My addiction prevented me from taking action. It didn't allow me to because I lied about the substance I was addicted to. I lied to myself about prescription medication. There was a solace in prescription medications that differed from other substances such as alcohol, narcotics, and the like. Simply put, I wasn't buying heroin off the corner of a street, which gave me comfort. This became the most dangerous lie, one that was the driving force and motivation behind reaching rock bottom.

Even now, in a completely different state and far removed from that time, I have realized for the first time in my life that this story, this attempt at providing light to others, is the first time I'm not trying to prove anything to anyone. I am motivated by serving what is best for MY future, MY desires, MY second chance. And as this story continues, the motivation of the purpose in life I later came to identify becomes clearer.

Insecurities and ego are inherent in our DNA. The difference lies in identifying that those two traits must never serve to motivate our actions.

As a result of knowing that, owning that, and battling myself to understand my own decision-making process by identifying my weaknesses and turning them into my strengths, my discipline has changed, and so should yours. I put aside my emotions and my feelings and focused on what needed to be fixed.

Within three months following my return to my childhood home, without the medications that kept me from giving my body the nutrition that I needed, I instantly gained weight. My body went into defense mode, storing everything I consumed, having been deprived of nutrition for so long due to the side effects of Adderall. I was never hungry. I never ate. Pills were all I consumed.

In November of 2018, just three months off the medication and living with my parents, I went from 160 pounds to an all-time high of 235 pounds. I was too weak at this point to even think about working out. I was on a journey to build the discipline necessary to wake up without a pill and to fall asleep without one. These were the toughest months, both physically and mentally, and the side effects of such extreme weight gain only made it worse. Even in my recovery, I lied to myself about my weight gain and the reason I was there. However, this time, I immediately recognized this lie, this excuse for the weight gain. It was me. My lack of physical activity. That was the bottom line. That was the simple truth.

Truth may be a battle of perceptions, but when it comes to the truths you know about yourself, there is but one perception: yours. Take a good, hard look in the mirror and understand that where you are physically is a result of your actions or lack thereof.

You know, we live in a new era where our primary concerns often revolve around social media and the outward projections we make, along with those perceptions I mentioned earlier in the battle for the truth. What are these outward projections? What do people think of us? But why do we care? How do they control or affect where and what you do with your life? I have no pity for any circumstance, not because I lack empathy or compassion, but because life has taught me that the only consequences of tomorrow are determined by me today. The only way I can be sure I'm making the right decisions is if I understand why I am making those decisions. You're going to confront some hard truths, things that maybe you don't want to accept about yourself. But if you don't at least address them, how can you work past them? How will you ever find an opportunity to become the best version of yourself if you don't understand what motivates your behavior?

When we allow our emotions to control our responses, we've already failed. My denials with prescription medication, my perception of a doctor's office, and prescription medication justified my use, my abuse, and my overmedication. While these medications certainly altered my perceptions and my abilities, to be clear in my thought process, there's one thing I did know for certain: I was taking these pills to hide from the realities of my life.

Instead of trying to work through issues, I didn't want to confront them. I just wanted to hide away from them. I wished for some sort of miracle to happen, that suddenly everything would change. And I can promise you that will never happen. There isn't just a snap of the fingers and your problems are gone. That's where we have to begin. That's where we have to start our journey of finding ourselves by understanding who we really are, why we are the way we are, and understanding the motivations that led to my failures and eventually overcoming those tragic events that I thought would define me for the rest of my life.

There were moments following my addiction and overdose when I felt like I was wearing a scarlet letter, as if I was permanently scarred by this tragic time in my life, one that I could never overcome or get over. And once again, I wasn't focusing on myself. This outward appearance, which causes so much concern, serves us with nothing. These feelings of shame and regret consumed me following my overdose, but those feelings wouldn't change anything. My past would not change. I had already learned that allowing my feelings to control my decisions caused me to lose all reason. The guilt I felt for the damage I created was understandable; it means I have a conscience.

Regret and shame, those feelings don't serve me today, nor do they serve my future. I knew I had to make that change. I would no longer engage in any activity, conduct, or thought that did not serve me.

I was in my head, thinking I'd ruined everything: my career, my future, my friendships – they were all gone at that point. And I didn't know what to do. But I knew I had to face it head-on, and that's where it began. Owning what led me there, understanding what motivated me to get there, and saying I'm never going back there. And I did so slowly because if there's one thing in any attempt to overcome adversity, tragedy, or failure, or what may be perceived as life-altering moments in our life, you have to be easy on yourself. You have to take it slow, one step at a time.

But how can you know what step to take if you don't identify what needs to be fixed? For me, immediately outward, I knew I needed to change my health. Physically, I needed to get myself stronger again. I had brought myself to a point where I couldn't sleep without a pill or wake up without a pill. How could I do that now? How could I even get to work?

Physically exhausted and recovering from substance abuse did not excuse the obligations required to repair my business. I could no longer lie that my business was destroyed by anything other than me. This accountability was important, but the actions that followed and motivated me to repair had to be taken with care, caution, precision, and patience.

In the beginning, knowing my limitations, I did so slowly. For the first month, I would only work a few hours a day. In time, that would develop into full working days created by implementing consistent daily disciplines.

I set personal and professional standards. I made commitments to work out weekly and to address a number of files daily. I was determined to no longer be motivated by lies but motivated by the reality before me.

I became motivated to heal, to repair, and to strengthen what was so weak. I began this physical discipline by scheduling my workouts in my calendar to keep myself accountable. I did it slowly, starting with three times a week, then four times a week. Gradually, I became stronger. I felt myself caring about myself rather than trying to prove myself. Physical activity became necessary not only to strengthen but also to repair. I began to test my capacity instead of lying to myself and depriving myself of my abilities. Suddenly, the need for sleep was something my body craved—it needed rest because I was engaged. My mind no longer raced in bed with unnecessary thoughts.

All the damage I had done to my business—the disorganization, the deep financial hole I put my office in—needed immediate attention. I was focused on getting organized and in order, but again, it was one step at a time. And I did it. The three-hour workdays immediately became six-hour workdays, and then the clock became irrelevant. I was encouraged, I was motivated, and I saw changes. I took on each issue task by task and fixed what needed to be done.

So many of my failures were driven by insecurities that I chose not to address. I chose to ignore or allow my ego to say, "No, not me." When you fail to acknowledge your own issues, when you fail to acknowledge your own behaviors, you'll never see past the adversity and failure that you may find yourself in right now. You blind yourself from reality. But, nothing changes if nothing changes. More importantly, change cannot occur without understanding the motivations that led you to where you are.

The story of privilege I shared motivated my demise. Was I no longer good enough? Did I not deserve the friends and family I had if not for those material burdens? None of that matters. The reality is that there is no reason to have such concern. The fear of exposure that I meddled with, and the outward appearance that I was no longer capable of projecting, motivated my failures. Those fears cause you to hide and deny the truth of what the struggle actually is—the disaster that is being created.

When the response to insecurities is motivated by ego, the result leads to one's demise. My ego drove me to these failures, to making these wrong decisions that eventually led to the compounded chaos I put myself through.

That battle with yourself, self-awareness, self-defeat, all of it—it's about you. The reason we self-sabotage is that it allows us to predict what is going to happen. It gives the illusion of self-control.

Nobody's put you in this adversity that you find yourself in. And if you are in a difficult space, your response to that has to serve you. And if you believe your ego serves you, I can promise you it doesn't. It's masking instead of dealing. And that's where we go next.

CHAPTER 3

The Effect of Masking, Instead of Dealing

I had no other option, no other choice. Open the law firm, save my family's business, give them everything they had given me. This was my time, the prodigal son, the opportunity to fix what was not my failure because of the burdens I felt for the privileges I was given. I walked into the door of that amazing condo I once had, and I no longer saw the tile on the floor. Every single space on the floor, no matter where in that apartment, was covered with papers.

I had no idea what to do, but I took each part in turn. All while dealing with an eviction, complete financial failure, and suddenly a responsibility not only to take care of myself but my family and their business. I was so distracted. To give me the power, the strength, at least I thought, to make this happen. So, pills became my miracle drug. The limitless pill that I convinced myself wouldn't let me fail. That would allow me to keep going, and then I was sure to succeed. But what I ignored, what I didn't address, was the overwhelming toll on myself in mind and body.

It was all-consuming, and I didn't want to know or deal with the real struggle—depression, anxiety, the overwhelming nature of all of this happening at one time while saying to myself, *Don't forget you had so much promise; you have to make sure to become that person you promised yourself you would be.* Well, that was too much to deal with in the midst of trying to deal with all the others. That doctor's office became my safe space. The piece of paper I would receive before walking out of that office took just five minutes to get. Its purpose was nothing more than to shield myself, to hide my own thoughts, and, more importantly, to avoid facing what was actually my reality.

The dependency I began to develop wasn't simply because these drugs have addictive qualities but because my mind required me to escape so I didn't have to deal. Prescriptions became my mechanism, my masking mechanism. And how dangerous that is, how dangerous that can become when the idea of life in and of itself, the fragility of it, knowing just how fragile our lives are, the one opportunity that we only know, no matter what your faith may be, I tried to escape.

The truth is, this is our one shot at life. This is what we have. Masking for me became so dangerous that I failed to appreciate the most fundamental privilege we all have—life and opportunity today. Right now, in this very moment, the opportunity to change and to be committed to change is now.

Masking your issues, not dealing with what is going on, will keep you distracted from the issues at hand. I became a hamster on a wheel, not because I wasn't working, but because my mind was controlled by medication. My decision-making and all my conduct were controlled by my substance abuse.

Two hundred milligrams of Adderall in a day was a walk in the park; 3 milligrams of Xanax to go to bed was the only way I could sleep. The body pain I developed I can never forget. I remember it like yesterday. My joints would crack by the simple movement of my arm from one direction to the next. I developed such bad nerve pain that I felt paralyzed.

Instead of dealing, I was masking all of the personal, financial, and professional issues that were actually at the center of my circumstance. This was only made worse by masking the effects of my addiction. The side effects of overuse manifested themselves in my mind and body. I couldn't wake up without a pill. I couldn't sleep without a pill. But, once I was awake, I needed more pills than the one or two required to get out of bed. The high wore off, and I needed more. There was work to do, and my mind believed another pill would get the work done, not me.

The problem was I had yet to do any work. Instead, I was just focusing on suddenly feeling that body pain that came right back. I just spent six hours of my day looking at a prescription bottle. The masking caused me to believe, *Without this pill, you can't do this.* I no longer became capable of anything but dependent on prescription medication to escape my reality.

And by the time the pill took over, the pain that I experienced physically, truly physically, couldn't be avoided. It was my only focus. So, another pill for another reason. I had to take something to avoid the restlessness of my muscles. The Lorazepam was that, and then it was another medication. Well, suddenly, I'm talking about the stresses of life and telling this doctor I can't deal, and Prozac is now what's on the table, and anti-suicide medication was. I said yes. I needed it in my mind. I needed all of them. The reality is I did not need them for any other reason than to hide. I needed them to avoid the external pressures that I thought controlled my outcome when, in reality, my outcome was being controlled by my substance abuse.

My choice to continue to hide, to mask, to avoid by taking pills--being so caught up in my feelings rather than my actions. That was why I got to where I was. My business was not failing for any other reason than me. The lack of attention, organization, and success was all created because I did not face things head-on.

I tried moving around things instead of moving through things. These are disciplines that require effort and consistent work on a daily basis that will not be easy to achieve or miraculously bestowed upon you. To accomplish actual change, to make an impact in your future that will lead to attaining the goals you seek, requires a relentless effort towards identifiable, tangible tasks.

The disaster I created in business from my substance abuse led me to mix client files, spending settlement funds to move the costs on other cases. I commingled client funds just to keep things going. There was no life of privilege, no benefit to me directly. I did not get to live some lavish life. I was broke. My business was destroyed, and just to keep the lights on in my business and to move client case files forward, I mixed everything. I own that.

Commingling client funds is not something I had to confront lightly. It is not something to be taken lightly. For my business, in my recovery, this was the single most important task. I confronted this head-on and was determined to get out of this financial disaster. I knew that the lack of organization, the lack of focus, and the excuses that led to my lies required me to identify each issue and correct it.

Dealing with this professional and ethical failure was the single most difficult thing I faced. The single most important issue that required immediate attention. It required action. I acted. I identified the issues, and I ensured I got things in order. I realized that what I was able to correct, without excusing the professional and ethical failure, came from direct action. I maintained my client's trust and confidence in the years that followed because I acted. This action did not originate from an authoritative body demanding it, nor from a client complaint. Instead, it stemmed from my own effort, commitment, and dedication to no longer mask, but to confront and address the issue.

I had enough of the "what if" in my mind and the shame. Those feelings also could no longer be masked. Frankly, the feelings did not matter. My clients did not deserve that, Olga did not deserve that, and neither did I. Being committed to dealing with the problems of life requires a relentless effort and dedication to never mask, make excuses, or avoid what is actually in your control.

In the same vein that I would need to confront the issues I created from my addiction, so too would I need to confront the depression, guilt, and fear my mind felt.

This time, however, I was afraid. The idea of talk therapy, a mental health professional, may lead me right back to prescription medication. Initially, this is what I truly believed, and I used it as an excuse not to get proper mental health care. My dedication to physical fitness provided me with the mental therapy that I needed at the time. My body built mental strength through that physical effort, but I now know that talk therapy is critical and will always advocate for anyone who has dealt with or is dealing with substance abuse to obtain proper mental health care treatment. Thankfully, along with my physical fitness routine, I had a support system from family and friends that allowed me to be vulnerable about my past and about my feelings.

My greatest support came from my paternal grandmother, whom I called Teta. She was my everything, but passed away in January 2021. Prior to her passing, but after my overdose, the relationship I developed with her as her health was ailing would be my greatest source for forgiving myself.

She was a committed woman of faith and had worked in the Orthodox Church her entire life. She could recite bible verses perfectly from memory. Her greatest lesson to me was about forgiveness. This is how she taught me to deal. This is how I learned not to mask the feelings of shame and regret that would follow my overdose.

There was one specific day that I asked her what was the best lesson she could teach me with respect to forgiveness. She responded, "This is the best question you can ask because they asked Jesus Christ himself this same question. She went on to recite Matthew 18:21-22: *"Then Peter came to Jesus and asked, 'Lord, how many times shall I forgive my brother when he sins against me? Up to seven times?' Jesus answered, 'I tell you, not seven times, but seventy-seven times.'"*

The forgiveness she recollected must come from within, must come from the heart. We never talked about my addiction, my overdose, my failures—but she knew—she always knew. And in her way, she taught me to be easy on myself, to find forgiveness within my own heart as Jesus taught his disciples.

And that's what you need to know—to move forward—to truly no longer mask what is holding you from moving forward—you must forgive yourself. You must take accountability and move forward with discipline. Not just words, but action.

You must give yourself hope. What is hope? What is encouragement? It is an experience that blows away the clouds of doubt and disappointment so that the light of our spirit can shine through.

The circumstances you find yourself in today are not a result of anything other than your own conduct. It's not to say that people don't experience events like the loss of employment or the tragic death of a loved one, possibly for reasons beyond their control. There is no doubt that such events occur. However, the event itself doesn't matter as much as the response to what happens.

That response, the choices made that follow, the decision to act today, to pursue what you desire, will determine what tomorrow will be. Masking and not dealing will only hold you back and prevent you from achieving what you set out for. What requires your attention is not going to change by anything other than the choices that you make. That was hard to understand, to come to accept because now there wasn't an excuse.

Now, I had no more pills to take. The fact that my body suddenly weighed over 230 pounds was due to no one but myself. I had to confront it. So, I made choices. I implemented a daily discipline, starting with 30 minutes of cycling five times a week. This routine led to changes not only in my body but also in my mind. I was no longer masking or making excuses, but rather facing my challenges head-on. The visible physical changes in my body were encouraging. The motivation to persevere and the resilience I built stemmed from my actions—my daily discipline—the standard from which I would not deviate, regardless of the day's challenges. This was how I chose to respond.

This commitment to my physical health would be the foundation for changes that would make me far more capable than I ever imagined. The commitment to my physical health gave me the strength to deal with the stressors of work and the failures I needed to address in business. The dependence on prescription medication was no longer a thought but a distant memory of a life I was determined to overcome. That determination became the inspiration for being so open about my addiction, my abuse, and my attempt to take my own life.

In 2019, I chose to discuss these issues publically, through social media, and through a podcast—exposing my failure to the world in the most public of ways. I did not need to mask or hide from my past; I needed to inspire. These were all choices that I made to confront anything and everything that was holding me back.

These were choices that made changes, albeit slowly, but I set out to change my life. I wasn't a victim. I was a victim of my own self. And I had to come to realize that this constant use of prescription medication was because I chose that life. I kept putting Band-Aids on issues in an effort to mask my reality. Pills were my Band-Aid. The Band-Aid to have the energy and focus, all the clarity and ability to be successful. I was responsible for this lie and for the conduct I engaged in to mask instead of deal.

I realized that from 2016 to 2018, my suffering, my pain, and the disaster I found myself in were all due to my own actions. It was a hard pill to swallow, a difficult truth to accept. I had to confront it.

Confronting these challenges is the only way forward, no matter how daunting it may seem. No matter how insurmountable the mountain appears to be, it's okay. I can assure you it's okay. You have reached the lowest point; there's nowhere else to go.

But is that what you truly believe? Ask yourself honestly, do you believe that? This rock bottom that seems impossible to overcome, this life-altering, defining moment has not irrevocably decided your fate and your future.

If that's something that you think is true, I can promise you that you are wrong. You are far more capable. We are far more capable. I came to learn that through physical fitness and focus on my mind. We'll talk about that. But now is the time to take a good, hard look at why you are where you are and own it. Own you. No one's going to change your circumstance for you but you.

So what do you do? Are you masking? Are you avoiding it? Are the external pressures that you think are so influential and impactful on your life the decision-makers of your future? They're not. I know they're not.

Even as time went on, and I thought I was so far from this period of time, the years that it took to fix all the mistakes that I made in my business and life, personally, professionally, and financially, came back to hit me hard, harder than you could ever imagine. Still, I chose to deal.

I chose to be the decision maker of my future by dealing with the issue head-on, not going around it, but going through it. That's the only way. I promise you, it's the only way, even if you've overcome rock bottom and you find yourself struggling again. Saying, why me? Why now? I've already gone through it. I've already overcome it. That is simply a test of the resilience you have built. A test of your ability to deal and no longer mask.

Don't fall back. Don't resort back to the behaviors that led you there in the first place. I continue to learn that now. I'm learning that as I'm writing this here. That's what you need to know. That's what you have to ask yourself in your journey to overcome whatever it may be that you're going through in any area of your life.

Deal with the issues, set goals, and implement disciplines that address whatever it may be. Not by avoiding or masking or finding a substance or anything else for that matter that will allow you to escape the reality that lies before you. It takes time. But I can promise you, from my own experiences, if there's one thing life has taught me, it's that those external pressures, those issues, they're never going to go away. They may be different. They may be more harmful, more impactful, harder to get through, and a bigger struggle. It's life.

That's what life is about. But your response, the way you address it, and how you deal with it, will be the reason that you get through it. Remember, our circumstances, our lives, are in our control. The future you seek is simply determined by the conduct that you choose to engage in. At the end of the day, you are always one decision away from a totally different life. But you have to choose that different life. You have to take action.

I decided to deal. First, I had to find the strength. I found that through fitness, and my God, did it serve me. I no longer needed those pills that I thought I needed to change my mood and mask my mental health issues.

There is no doubt that the effects of psychotropic medications alter your mood and cause significant changes in your serotonin and dopamine levels. Now imagine if you can get that satisfaction, you can deal with that stress, you can become stronger internally through your own inner strength, through your body and what it is capable of. There is nothing stronger. There is nothing more capable of overcoming adversity than the human body. It is built with the ability to have the strength to endure.

Physical fitness gave me strength, and it can give you strength. Fitness allowed me to cope with stress and external pressures that I would continue to be confronted with. It became an outlet. It became a mechanism to find stability. And most importantly, it gave me the confidence to know that the foundation I sought, the stability I required, must come from within. The same holds true for you. We're all the same. We are all human. We're all capable of failure. We all do fail. The difference between us is our reactions, our decisions, and the choices that we make. Only you can determine that. Once you know that, you must then identify your purpose.

CHAPTER 4

No Purpose, No Future

To control your path forward and obtain the future that you desire, you must first find your purpose. You must identify the purpose that ignites your vision to succeed and to become the best version of yourself. Identifying that purpose will be the driving force to remaining committed to daily disciplines that make the most out of each and every day.

Identifying a purpose is important to building a successful future because it provides direction, motivation, and a sense of fulfillment. Here are a few reasons why identifying a purpose is important:

- *Direction*: Having a clear purpose helps you set goals and make decisions that are aligned with your values and aspirations. It guides you towards a specific path, saving time and energy by focusing on what truly matters to you.

- *Motivation*: A purpose gives you a reason to wake up every morning with enthusiasm and drive. It provides motivation to overcome challenges and setbacks along the way, as you have a deeper meaning and long-term vision driving your actions.

- *Resilience*: When faced with obstacles or setbacks, a strong sense of purpose can help you stay resilient and persevere. It provides a reminder of why you started in the first place and keeps you resilient in times of adversity.

- *Meaning and fulfillment*: Having a purpose allows you to find meaning in your actions, as you are working towards something that aligns with your values and passions. This sense of fulfillment can lead to greater overall satisfaction and happiness in life.

- *Impact*: A purpose-driven life often involves making a positive impact on others and society as a whole. By identifying a purpose, you can contribute to the greater good, make a difference in the world, and leave a lasting legacy.

The future you desire must come from a purpose you identify. Identifying a purpose is important for building a successful future because it provides direction, motivation, resilience, meaning, and opportunity to make a positive impact. It allows you to live a fulfilling life that aligns with your values and passions.

The fire that drives your being and allows you to remain committed to accomplishing those daily tasks builds the confidence necessary to endure. That sense of accomplishment, in turn, lays the foundation for the future you wish to build. A future constructed on a relentless pursuit of greatness, proven through daily effort. Your purpose can emerge from trauma, as it did for me, or through unique personal experiences that offer motivation tailored to you. This cannot be determined by anyone but yourself. Mark Twain said, "The two most important days in your life are the day you are born, and the day you find out why." The latter serves as the discovery of your purpose.

For me, those two days are May 7, 1990, and July 11, 2018. My birthdate and the day I was given a second chance at life. A reflection now that turned failure, a cataclysmic self-inflicted catastrophe, into a moment of enlightenment. A realization of the purpose I have moving forward.

July 11, 2018. A day I'll never forget, but somehow can't remember clearly. That's the effect of an overdose, but it gave me purpose. The purpose is to make an impact in this world and to take advantage of the second chance at life I was given by serving my community, advocating in the space of mental health and substance abuse, and, above all, becoming dedicated to my craft and my business in a way I never have before.

I established a standard in my life by embracing my second chance. The burdens of privilege from the life I once knew transformed from burdens into my standard. Now, I recognize the blessing of the life once given to me; it set the minimum standard for the life I want to create for myself. This change in perspective was crucial because it no longer held me back but inspired me to achieve greatness. Now, I can provide for my family while still caring for myself. Finding purpose in life is critical to moving forward and taking advantage of the second chance you can create out of your life.

The only thing I do know, the one thing I knew so vividly and so clearly from that day, was sitting in the back of that taxi and opening up that bag with the prescriptions inside faster than the gearshift went from park to drive. I remember it like yesterday. I also remember so vividly, so clearly, somehow coming to and seeing my father and Felicia at the edge of that hospital bed.

I fell so fast. I couldn't believe it. In that very moment when I was filled with shame, I was also filled with rage, disappointment, and failure. I was so angry that it didn't work, taking my life, that is. I kept asking myself, *Why do I have to deal with this issue again?* I couldn't deal with it in that moment while getting a second opportunity and chance at life. I pulled the IVs out of my arm and fled. How selfish. Honestly, it was pathetic. I knew it. But what I didn't know at that time was how selfish my addiction was to the people around me.

Our actions carry consequences not only for ourselves but also for those around us. In my case, cutting everyone out of my life, destroying my business, and losing complete focus—the compounded chaos I created through substance use and abuse was incredibly selfish. I needed to take responsibility. I had to own it. The awareness that my consideration of suicide, driven by selfishness, could profoundly impact my friends and family, motivated me to accept responsibility for these relationships and strive to mend them. The harm I caused myself had potentially far-reaching and incalculable effects on others.

My second chance at life instilled in me a purpose. Often, when we face what we perceive as catastrophic failure, we seek someone to blame. It's easier to avoid taking responsibility. But I had no choice. At 28 years old, I had to move back home. I wasn't a man; I was a child in need of his parents' care.

Getting caught with medication as I tried to enter a rehab center, with it hidden in my suitcase, illustrated just how far I had fallen. That moment made me realize the harm was self-inflicted. The external pressures I ignored, the people I cut out of my life, my disregard for those affected, like Olga, whom I was privileged to have in my life—none of these mattered due to the selfishness of my addiction.

The changes you wish to see, the ones we all want to make, the downfall you want to avoid, must originate from within. There's no other way. I thought I would be ashamed of my addiction, that I needed to hide from everyone and everything because of the chaos I caused. But this time, I made a decision. I chose to start a podcast and talk about my struggles. To tell my story openly, vividly, so raw, and honestly, but also publicly. I decided to take control, deciding that my outcome wouldn't be predetermined. I chose to speak the truth, not for anyone else but for myself. That was the lesson I needed. I found purpose in failure.

Life teaches us through errors. When we accept the lessons from our failures and our mistakes with humility and gratitude, we grow that much more. We find purpose. I realized an opportunity came from my failures—an opportunity to make an impact on others.

I needed to talk it out, even if it meant public scrutiny. There was a measure of accountability that would serve others. Even as a lawyer and as a professional, sharing such personal failure could lead to helping others in this field who struggle similarly.

Doing so in this way also served to prevent me from turning back to prescription medication. I never wanted to go back to that self-inflicting, harmful behavior by letting everyone know what happened so it would never happen again. My purpose in life, the driving force behind my recovery, what allowed me to be stronger, also made me accountable. I knew that to be stronger, I had to own my behavior and my conduct. Not just mentally and physically but in every other area of my life.

This was done to prevent the same downfall from happening again. It leads us to the question of why we fall and why we become so consumed with harmful, self-destructive behaviors. What a joy that was. The authenticity of the revelations that I made. The honesty with my mental health struggle. The understanding and compassion I now have for people who have gone through similar struggles are immense. Struggling with addiction, suicidal thoughts, failures in life, business, and family relationships. There I was, at 28 years old, with lessons of failure most people my age have never experienced, having lost everything all at once. And instead of working to improve their lives, many turn to substances, worsening their situation to the point where life itself becomes unbearable.

Now, I know my purpose. If I had understood these lessons earlier, perhaps I wouldn't have fallen as hard as I did. The possibility of offering someone, even just one person, a glimmer of hope and preventing them from falling, as I did, motivates me to this day.

To realize, to share, to encourage the idea that the power of changing, the power of dealing, what is really holding us back is ourselves, is the purpose that drives me.

I will always maintain, from my own experience, that addiction is never solely about the substance we choose. It's about the mental health struggles we face and what we are trying to escape from. But more importantly, it's about how quickly we can fall and how much harm we can inflict, not by anyone else's doing but by our own.

The most difficult thing to accept is that our current state, what we want, and the changes we need to make are not dictated by external pressures that may influence our thoughts and actions but rather by ourselves.

Where are you in your life now? Are you where you want to be? Ask yourself truly. If the answer is no, now ask yourself why. The only answer to that question is you.

I came to this realization through the second chance I gave myself. It wasn't handed to me by someone else; I chose to seize that second chance. The true blessing was waking up in that hospital, even if I didn't want to be there at the time. That was a gift I had been given—an opportunity I would never take for granted again.

I was resolute in my belief that downfall and failure would never be options because I chose for them not to be. The key is to choose. You always have to make decisions that improve the outcome of tomorrow, even when it seems impossible or improbable. But why? Because even when you think you've overcome it, even when you think you've dealt with it and you're so far from what you have now overcome, I promise you, you will learn as I did that life will hit you again.

But how strong have you become from those failures? What did you learn from that downfall? Are the decisions you're making now with that in mind? Or are you reverting back to the same behaviors that led to the initial failure?

I asked myself this question just two months ago when I felt lost in my thoughts, fearing a downfall was imminent six years later. I realized then that I would be the only person determining my future and success. I remembered that period well—the darkness, the loneliness, and how weak my body and mind were, leading to my failures.

That promise I made to myself was crucial: to never allow anything or anyone but my own actions to dictate my future. Why? The answer is simple: You don't truly appreciate life until you're afraid of losing it. I vowed never to live in fear again. I had already received a second chance, and no matter what came my way, I knew I would never take it for granted again.

In identifying my purpose, I identified the force that would motivate me to embrace my second chance at life. That purpose revealed my full potential.

CHAPTER 5

A Second Chance

This is it. This is your fucking moment. You are not defined by what's happened to you. You are what you do.

What does that mean? Who gets to decide if you get a second chance? Those are the questions I had in my head. Those are the things that I wondered about immediately after moving back into my parents' house. I didn't know if I would ever come back, but I knew if I did, I would be the only one who would determine if I'd have a second chance. The responsibility fell entirely on me: the responsibility to myself, my family, friends, clients, employees, and really, to anyone.

I took ownership. I am accountable. Not just for how far I had fallen, but for how far I would grow. I learned the consequences of allowing my thoughts to dictate my behavior. I realized the effect of external pressures influencing my daily discipline. From then on, I made a commitment to myself that I would never again allow external pressures or internal thoughts to control me.

In my recovery, in the months that followed, with the weight gain I sustained, my mindset did not shift. To this day, that mindset, the discipline that I committed to following my overdose, is unwavering.

The standard that I set for myself—the dedication to my health, fitness, nutrition, and mental health—that I committed to would be the foundation of my resilient strength. The second chance I embraced is mine to control even when tested years later.

My road to recovery, my second chance, would begin with the one thing I needed most—stability, internally and externally, in mind and body. I developed that stability through a daily commitment to engaging in physical fitness. I realized that in doing so, I became internally stable—literally, my core, my abdominals, and my legs. That stability and strength transcended physicality into my mind, building a stronger, more formidable mental state than I have experienced before.

A dedication to and focus on physical fitness naturally creates a strong mind, but they require patience and consistent effort. My fitness journey began with a simple cardio routine and has since developed into a more rigorous protocol, including weight lifting, cardio, and high-intensity interval training at least six days a week. Even on rest days, I choose to move my body with a simple walk on the treadmill. The benefits of simply moving your body cannot be understated.

My greatest strength, the biggest changes that I witnessed, occurred when I began training with a close friend, Joe. Joe is a mammoth of a human being. He is the definition of being physically fit, standing at 6'7", a renowned trainer and former boxer. I admired him before knowing the impact he would have on my life. There was a unique bond that we shared, that he understood, given my substance abuse.

While his story is not mine to tell, he understood me. He cared about my progress and my fitness journey in a way that I had yet to know. He taught me patience. He was aggressive, forceful, and demanding of my efforts. His routines incorporated intense, constructive critique that required me to dig deep and test my physical limits in ways I had never done before. He made me accountable by leaving it to me to track my progress. He hated the scale and taught me not to let it be my measure, but to actually measure myself. And I did.

There it was. The consequence of discipline. The consequence of an unwavering commitment to hitting your goals. I no longer measured my success by a single number on a scale. I dug deep and appreciated the second chance at life that I not only knew, but was encouraged by Joe to take full advantage of. I remember telling him that my body, genetically, was just not capable of a 6-pack. An unrealistic goal that genetically I was prohibited from attaining. I was wrong.

I remembered the promise I made to myself. I remembered that I would not let my inner thoughts dictate my behavior. I remembered my promise. I remembered my commitment to never let external pressures or internal thoughts dictate my behavior. Within two years, I didn't just reach my goal. I surpassed it. I continued to test my limits. I ran two half-marathons and completed the Chicago triathlon. I wouldn't go so far as saying I am an athlete because my hand-eye coordination is still shit, but physically I am at my best.

Even when tested and under pressure professionally, I maintained and continue to maintain a level of dedication to my physicality that has directly benefited me professionally and, most importantly, mentally. That dedication has led to a body fat percentage of sub-7%, and I have maintained that for over two years now—something I could have never imagined. I have always fluctuated in weight since childhood, but not anymore.

Physical fitness builds strong character for several reasons:

- *Discipline*: Regular exercise requires commitment, consistency, and self-discipline. By incorporating physical fitness into one's routine, individuals develop the discipline necessary to set goals, work hard, and stay focused on achieving them. This discipline translates into other areas of life, such as work, relationships, and personal growth.

- *Determination*: Physical fitness often involves pushing oneself beyond comfort zones and overcoming challenges. Through exercise, individuals learn to face adversity, persist in the face of difficulties, and develop mental resilience. This builds a strong character based on determination and perseverance.

- *Confidence*: Engaging in regular physical activity boosts self-confidence and self-esteem. As individuals improve their physical fitness levels, they become more aware of their capabilities and strengths, which positively impacts their overall confidence. This increased self-confidence can extend to other aspects of life, promoting strong character founded on self-belief and assertiveness.

- *Emotional well-being*: Physical fitness has numerous mental health benefits, such as reducing stress, anxiety, and depression. Regular physical activity releases endorphins, which are natural mood-boosting chemicals in the brain. When individuals prioritize physical fitness, they are more likely to experience improved mental well-being, leading to greater emotional stability and resilience.

- *Personal responsibility*: Physical fitness requires individuals to take personal responsibility for their health and well-being. By making choices that prioritize exercise and overall fitness, individuals develop a sense of accountability and self-care. This sense of personal responsibility extends beyond physical fitness and helps build strong character traits like accountability, integrity, and autonomy.

- *Teamwork and cooperation*: Engaging in physical activities often involves collaboration and cooperation, especially in team sports or group exercises. Building physical fitness can strengthen social bonds and promote teamwork. Learning to work as part of a team builds character traits such as cooperation, communication, and the ability to consider the needs and perspectives of others.

Physical fitness is critical in building strong character because it cultivates discipline, determination, confidence, emotional well-being, personal responsibility, and teamwork. These character traits lay the foundation for personal growth, success, and a healthy, fulfilling life. This is the basis for giving yourself a second chance.

The second chance I chose to give myself, the downfall I was coming out of, I now know was a blessing. That epiphany was a consequence of my actions, not words. My physicality didn't change simply because I worked out. Attention to my diet and what I consumed was critical. There can be no doubt that you are what you eat. Your daily calorie consumption, the types of food you eat, and the timing of when you eat that food will directly correlate to your progress. It's science, and it's simple if you choose to understand it.

I was no longer just eating to eat. Nonsense calories, or snacks here and there, were no longer desired. I wanted to fuel my body. I gave my body what it needed for energy. I began to plan and prepare my food in advance. This dedication was goal-oriented, it was focused, and it worked. The thought of the irreparable damage I had done to my body from my addiction was proven false by my action and my committed daily discipline. Incorporating a fasting routine to utilize the sources of energy within my body that may be stored was critical in this process. This aspect of my nutrition did not come until I was tested by the haunting consequences of my past.

Truthfully, I have always cared about my outward appearance. There's a lot underneath that, but I own that. I appreciate that. I think that builds confidence, and I don't think you should be ashamed of that. You should be proud to care about how you appear. It builds confidence. I've always thought that confidence worked against me for those who may judge my outward appearance as arrogance. But I didn't care what others thought anymore. For me, those who know me know my core. Those who know me don't misunderstand my confidence for arrogance, but frankly, none of that matters.

I had to focus on self-care. For the first time in my life, I realized more than ever compassion, empathy, and love. Just in the way I nurtured my body. That nurturing nurtured my mind. It taught me to love myself and to forgive myself. So there I began. I began forgiving myself, talking through what I had done to myself in a way that was transformative. I became dedicated not only to changing for myself and my future but also for the love I wanted and the energy I needed from those around me. This meant I was responsible for the energy I gave to them. That was my driving force.

Those burdens that I felt before became a blessing, an empowerment, a motivation for me, which confirmed within me that my desires and goals I can still make true if I just focused on finding a little stability motivated by the purpose I identified. One thing I think we all sometimes lack is that feeling of stability. But stability requires balance, although they are distinct.

In the physical sense, they certainly appear to be similar—but they are not, even if they can be displayed by a single movement. I am talking about stability and balance in LIFE.

Author Tom Robbins said, "True stability results when presumed order and presumed disorder are balanced. A truly stable system expects the unexpected, is prepared to be disrupted, waits to be transformed." My second chance taught me this.

In the years of my addiction and opening my practice, I always felt internally unstable, like the ground that I would be walking on was literally going to crack, and I was going to fall through, and it was an awful feeling inside. But that foundation that I was looking for, that stability on the ground that I desired, that I needed, that I thought would allow for me to be successful, had to come from within—from my core. My physical core, like my abdominal region, needed to be rock solid, all of it. And that strength and realization of internal stability came through fitness.

The stability I developed gave me balance. My second chance at life led to the distinction of prioritizing and balancing my personal and professional life. Both are priorities that require attention without impact from the other. Simply put, stress from one would not deter or alter the obligations of the other.

Everyone can have a goal; everyone can set out for a discipline. But when you find a passion and strength from a dedication to yourself, there is no greater feeling than that. That was my second chance. I realized that my internal stability in mind and body increased my capacity.

Now, I know that I could never fully dedicate myself to anyone—clients, friends, family, or a loved one—if I am not the best version of myself, with a routine that never fails. This discipline requires me to stay focused, irrespective of external factors. No matter the pressures resulting from everything I had destroyed, I needed to commit to making changes on a daily basis.

This dedication to a routine has created a shield, a protection from influence and distraction, which I naturally encounter. This shield is strengthened each day due to my relentless pursuit of embracing my second chance.

I felt it. I saw it. My body changed. I had never seen this before, not even in my youth. I never thought I was capable of seeing a physique that I always admired.

I no longer doubted myself. We all have doubts; we doubt ourselves, but we shouldn't. I learned that doubts are just excuses. They are the reason we don't reach our goals. It's not because we're incapable, but because we lack dedication. It's because we don't try consistently.

These are things you have to accept. It's called accountability. I had to be accountable, but my accountability extended far beyond my own personal, mental, and physical state. It also required focusing on the business and repairing what I had destroyed.

The mess I created, stemming from my lack of care, concern, and attention while being consumed by addiction, undoubtedly led to mistakes. Looking back, I wish I had been more focused. But what would dwelling in regret, shame, and guilt over the failures I created for myself achieve? Simply put, absolutely nothing. And sure, understanding and accepting that is hard, but it's essential for giving oneself a second chance.

Day by day, effort by effort, goal by goal, I had to identify all the issues I created in my office. From every single client file I neglected, to accounting issues, to my failure to manage my clients' case files properly, even to the point of confusing cases as if they were all one. What was I doing? Well, it didn't matter anymore. What mattered was the present: where I was, what was in front of me, and what I needed to address and fix. Facing things head-on took time, a lot of time, and I was okay with that. I was patient with myself because real changes don't happen overnight.

Accepting this was tough. I had to learn to deal with stress in a new, focused, and direct way. Identifying the issues, understanding the goal, finding discipline, and making it happen. Sure, setting an alarm clock and waking up at five in the morning, getting to the gym by six, and ensuring I got my hour in before heading to the office was part of the routine. But it was much more than that.

It was about building a new discipline, one dedicated to my health, one that gave me internal strength and a release from external pressures and stressors in ways I hadn't focused on before. In those moments, months, and years that followed, my mind grew stronger. My desires, what I wanted to achieve, and my limits changed.

All of my goals (even the ones that I had before I opened my office) before I even became a lawyer were suddenly not enough. Even in the year or two before writing this, that goal seems like such a distant memory. It feels like step one in a game of 10 steps. We are far more capable than we could ever imagine. The only reason for that blindness is from failure to try. If you don't try, if you don't fail, you don't know.

We can't find a new path, greater success, or a different life for ourselves unless we do the work to get there. That was power. That was the strength that I needed. Failure became my greatest lesson. Those thoughts, those memories, those distant, distant memories of not being able to get up in the morning without a pill, to go to bed without a pill is ridiculous.

I laugh at it now. I only laugh because I had it in me the whole time. I didn't give myself enough credit. But that's okay. My failures, which were highly public due to my profession in law, where openly discussing addiction, overdose, and suicide attempt is considered taboo, have become the foundation of my resilience. They are the basis of my experiences that guide me forward.

I built a foundation, knowing that the experiences that I had gone through made me stronger. That scarlet letter I was so afraid of, the one that kept me taking the medication to hide behind the scars of what I wasn't dealing with, those were badges in our life; while they may not define us, they do teach us. That's a blessing.

I am responsible for where I am today and where I'll be tomorrow. And the experience that I've gone through, the addiction that I put myself through, the focus and dedication to physical fitness that has built an internal stability that I could have never imagined, a person with goals whose ideas and desires are in a realm that I never thought possible, all of that came from internal stability.

That is why I tell this story. That is the impact. That knowledge, that foresight into the future for what you want tomorrow, requires that accountability. Taking responsibility for where you are and your circumstances; it's not because of anyone but you.

If you build an unshakeable foundation, you will realize your capacity and build the strength necessary to overcome anything. And let me tell you something: now, more than ever, as I sit here, I understand that this lesson has been the most important one I've learned. Life is not linear. We will always experience fluctuations: good days, bad days, financial hardships, professional challenges, relationship difficulties, and general hardships will continue to come to me, to you, and to those around us, now and in the future. I'll explain why, but I'll do that later.

During these days, these years, my response to stress, external pressures, and difficulties would determine the outcome of tomorrow. That second chance I longed for meant that my reaction to whatever I faced today would shape tomorrow.

The discipline, focus, and standard I set for myself now extend to every area of my life—personal, professional, financial, you name it. You see, I still have hard days. There are mornings when I don't want to get out of bed and days when work is overwhelming and responsibilities seem too great. But that doesn't mean my discipline changes.

That's the stability I'm talking about. I remain stable. I have found balance because, irrespective of those external pressures or stressors, my discipline remains constant. Even in the face of failure, even if it all turns out as bad as you think it will, how will you continue to persevere? How do you choose to respond? What actions do you take?

These are questions I've asked myself just in the last few months. I chose to persevere. I choose to persevere. I will continue to persevere. These are not just words. These are my actions daily. I know that I don't get to wake up one day and say all the bad is gone, or I'll just ignore it, and it'll go away.

Those were the lies that I told myself. But if I was giving myself a second chance, I knew that nothing was going to miraculously change my circumstances other than me. And the same holds true for you. That truth will triumph over any adversity that you face. A focus on your physical and mental well-being will give you the strength to endure. These are the things that I've realized in my efforts.

I challenge you to become high achieving, to be successful beyond measure, and, more importantly, to be an advocate in a space that I know far too well. And so we grow. We climbed. We achieve. There I was, building this level of resilience. A strength that I had never known.

What does resilience mean to you? The blessing and responsibility that comes with giving yourself a second chance requires a level of resilience that must constantly be tested. One that you have to endure like a gladiator in an arena. Proud of what you have gone through. Not ashamed, not guilty. Honest. Authentic. Resilient.

I am defined by my resilience. I am empowered by it. I was once asked, "Why would you use such a negative term to describe yourself? Resilience just means somebody who's just wrought with problems and constantly has to overcome them. So why would you have that negative energy in your space?"

Oh, how small-minded, I thought. Failure teaches us; it provides experience that no one else has, offering an opportunity to overcome challenges. Resilience became my badge of honor. My scars exist for a reason: they narrate the story of everything I had to overcome to become the amazing person we are all inherently capable of becoming. This motivated my second chance and equipped me with the skills to endure. Because even after many years past this addiction, life struck me in ways you could never imagine. The irony that will emerge in this story was a test of my discipline. It became a test to see if I truly gave myself a second chance.

CHAPTER 6

The Rise of Resilience

Resilience is the capacity to withstand or to recover quickly from difficulties. Toughness, some would say. That's the definition of resilience. My dedication to change, return to my office, and focus on my business built strength. The results that I desired came from within. I saw my office changing. I got everything in order. It took time. My body started changing. Physically, I saw it in the mirror like I'd never seen before. My confidence grew. My mind got stronger. My discipline remained the same.

I chose not to allow myself to be defined by my past, correcting the mistakes that I had made, owning the failures that I had gone through, and giving light by advocating in this space without fear of professional or personal judgment. Because inspiring, enlightening, or motivating others who may similarly struggle outweighed any negative impacts in my mind. 2020 felt amazing. I started to grow, and so did my practice. We increased our caseload and were retained on hundreds of new client matters. Some of my cases obtained national news recognition. My discipline, my dedication to my business, and to myself, and to fitness were paying off. I felt it. I saw it. I was so, so proud.

As I grew, I saw changes and knew that I could go further beyond the limits I once believed I was constrained to. My fitness routine and dedication to my health demanded more. I needed to challenge myself, not just through physical endeavors like a half-marathon or triathlon, but a different kind of physical challenge that also required mental strength. This is when my mindset about nutrition shifted.

The way I fueled my body was guided by an informed, well-thought-out diet designed to provide my body with the energy it needs. I was no longer eating just to eat but eating to fuel. This psychological shift in how I approached nutrition also changed my definition of diet. The term "diet" can be problematic as it is often perceived as something temporary—a short-term change in eating habits solely for the purpose of achieving weight loss goals. This approach and perspective on nutrition can be quite dangerous.

To truly make sustainable health and lifestyle changes regarding nutrition, your commitment must extend beyond the temporary. It must be a lifelong dedication to changing your lifestyle. A focus on health and well-being should never be temporary, nor should your view on nutrition. We often perceive "diets" as restrictive measures, and this mindset does not support long-term changes. By its very nature, the term "diet" sets us up for failure; it sounds restrictive, creates a false sense of deprivation, and fosters a yearning for more once we're "on the other side."

This psychological paradigm on nutrition sets you up for failure. In reality, when you begin to eat clean and stay away from unnecessary sugars, junk carbs, and the like, you will feel better within days. Put it this way—if you've ever been on a journey to eat clean and slipped up by having fast food, or maybe giving yourself a "break" because you "deserve it." So you then decide to eat unhealthy, maybe you go as far as getting fast food. Maybe you call it a "cheat meal." How did that make you feel? I bet it made you feel like shit. You are what you eat, and the body will make sure you know that. It's incredible how quickly the body will make you realize that even after just one "cheat meal," you can feel terribly ill. Do you want to know why? Because when you stop poisoning your body, you start to recognize the real poison.

The need for a "cheat meal" or the false sense of deprivation caused by the idea of a "diet" is just that—false. It's a lie. The best way to confront that lie is with action. Start with a meal plan and measure your serving size and food quantity. Make sure that you are incorporating protein, fats, and carbohydrates in a manner consistent with your fitness goals. Yes, it requires work. But, if you want anything in life, you better put in the work. With time, that work will pay dividends in the future.

Most importantly, you will learn that focusing on what you consume by actually making your meals will erase the false sense of deprivation when thinking of a "diet." With patience and dedication, the false notion of craving what was restricted will no longer be desired. This mind-shift in nutrition requires the same discipline and commitment as a fitness routine.

This means incorporating a well-balanced diet that provides your body with the nutrition it needs, depending on the time of the day. Mealtimes interact with the natural processes in the body, such as circadian rhythm. Timing meals and digestion in a way that avoids disruption of these other processes tends to yield better health outcomes.

While the best time to eat varies from person to person, and it is best to consult a health professional to address your specific goals, my experience taught me that a well-balanced breakfast of protein, carbs, and fats gave me energy throughout the day. On the other hand, what I consumed at night and the time I ate depended on when I would go to sleep. I do not eat at least two to three hours before bedtime. More importantly, my final meal of the day is heavy in protein and far less in carbohydrates than any other meal to avoid spiking insulin levels and disrupting my sleep schedule, which occurs when you consume carbs.

At the end of this book, I have provided a free nutrition guide to share my process, which may be helpful in starting your journey. The best way to adopt this methodology is to prepare your meals for the week in advance. This preparation means you'll spend less time each day thinking about what to eat, when to eat, or how much you've eaten. Preparation in any area of life is critical to success, and this is especially true when developing your most capable human form.

The truth is that no one can buy a fit and healthy body. No surgeon in the world can shape up for you; you have to do it yourself. That is within your control, and that is how you rise. You must put in the work day in and day out. The daily effort you commit to makes you stronger, more resilient, and more capable. In my opinion, getting in shape and becoming the fittest version of yourself is the ultimate sign of self-respect.

These health and physical fitness changes consequently led to benefits in my personal and professional life. Financially, things changed. I moved back downtown, and while I wasn't in a million-dollar condo anymore, I got back downtown on my own terms. I was able to take care of my business and become net positive in our monthly operations.

Social media, particularly Instagram, became an important tool for my journey, both physically and mentally. The public nature of social media provided accountability, so I utilized it to stay disciplined. Maybe that was a mistake, or perhaps I was trying to prove myself to others. Nonetheless, I developed strength by using that platform to stay accountable.

I was committed to showing my workout routine daily, every single morning. I was dedicated to sharing the benefits that focusing on my fitness provided me. I maintained that discipline in my physicality by using my platform to share the changes I experienced—changes that became evident over time, showcasing my relentless commitment. This became a source of accountability. I began to inspire others to start their fitness journey and shared benefits beyond the physical, visible changes that stem from a consistent workout routine. I felt better, my mind was stronger, and I became more capable and resilient than ever before. I tested myself beyond my preconceived limitations and found myself sharing these experiences in an effort to inspire others to implement similar fitness routines.

The rise I witnessed in my personal, professional, and financial life was directly correlated to my efforts in the gym. After exercising, you tend to move more throughout the day. Eating healthy makes you feel better and more productive. Eating well and exercising goes beyond physical benefits; your mental health and productivity skyrocket, too.

It's a fact. I know it. The reality is that daily exercise will teach you more about yourself than anyone or anything ever could. When you commit to doing something hard, like working out and moving your body, lifting weights, day after day, you transform. Forcing yourself to do something hard day after day transforms you.

Looking back on it now, trying to prove myself to others is the way I look at it. Now, there's greater strength in that, and I'll explain more of it. But it was still so effective for keeping me accountable, for making sure that daily discipline, those posts every single morning in the gym kept me accountable.

I went beyond fitness in my use of social media and even began sharing general knowledge of the law. It was informative. It was impactful. There was a new wave. This became a new marketing strategy. My law firm would thrive through the use of social media.

The days of static billboards and TV commercials felt inauthentic to me. I didn't want clients to hire me because of a billboard or a commercial; I wanted them to hire me for who I was and for what I had grown from and overcome. In personal injury law, the clients I deal with have gone through catastrophic injuries, unimaginable to many. I wanted them to know that I, too, had experienced harm, even if it was self-inflicted. I knew physical and mental suffering. I aimed to offer them a different kind of attorney—one who owns their failures and isn't ashamed of their past. You might think this approach would destroy my business.

Professionally, I was often told that I must be insane to talk about this. Those two years, 2016 to 2018, were not just a snapshot in time; they were my drive, my resilience, my strength, my courage. I became relatable to an audience because I was authentically myself. And things changed. Discipline maintained itself. Finally, I found strength in acknowledging that I deserved this because of the effort I was putting in. Of course, it took years to reach that point. I really messed up, and there was a lot to fix. I wanted to grow physically, mentally, and financially, and all of that had to come from within.

Not allowing myself to be defined by my past and correcting my mistakes required a level of discipline and focus, unswayed by what I thought others might think. Tackling one thing at a time. And so, I did. By 2021, I moved into a new house, and things were amazing. My social media was growing. I had more cases than ever before, and year after year, we achieved more than ever before.

COVID hit us hard. For a plaintiff's personal injury law firm that operates on a contingency basis, meaning we don't get paid unless the case is resolved, the business came to a halt when the courts shut down. Boy, was I tested. But I had been building the resilience to endure external pressures, even something as significant and severe to my business operations as a complete shutdown of the court process. If the courts are shut down and cases aren't being heard, there's no motivation for the defense to resolve matters. They'll let time pass. And that's exactly what happened.

This time, though, I was okay. I was prepared, focused, and disciplined. As a result, I persevered. We grew in the years when we were expected to fail. My law firm's growth led to my recognition as a "Rising Star," placing me in the top 2.5% of attorneys in the State of Illinois, not just for one year, but for five consecutive years. I was also named in the Top 40 under 40 by the National Trial Lawyers Association for three years in a row. Additionally, I received the "Emerging Leader" award from the Arab American Business and

Professional Association for my community service efforts and professional accomplishments.

Then, the worst imaginable thing happened—a true test of what I had built. How resilient was I? I am so grateful for the lessons learned from another simple mistake. The haunting consequences of my past surged forward at the height of my rise. The ultimate test. How resilient was I? Would I persevere?

These are questions to which I now know the answers: yes, of course. Because my discipline has remained consistent. My focus on fitness and my skills in mind and body, in my health, ensuring that I am giving the best version of myself by first being the best version of myself, has proven that to be true. I remained committed to my daily discipline because of my drive, the purpose I identified, and the second chance at life I would never take for granted, no matter the circumstance.

This is the rise that naturally comes from building a resilient character. Resilience helps you navigate through the challenges and setbacks that life inevitably presents.

Here are the reasons why resilience is so important:

- *Overcoming obstacles*: Resilient individuals are better equipped to overcome obstacles and bounce back from failures. Instead of being defeated by setbacks, they view them as opportunities for growth and learning.

- *Adaptability*: Resilience enables individuals to adapt to changing circumstances. In an ever-evolving world, being able to adjust and thrive in new situations is crucial for personal and professional success.

- *Mental and emotional well-being*: Resilience promotes mental and emotional well-being by helping individuals deal with stress, trauma, and adversity. People with this trait are better able to maintain a positive outlook, manage their emotions, and cope with difficult situations.

- *Increased productivity and performance*: Resilient individuals tend to be more motivated and driven to achieve their goals. They have a determined mindset that allows them to stay focused and consistently perform at a high level, even in the face of challenges.

- *Stronger relationships:* Resilient individuals are often more compassionate and understanding towards others. They can offer support and be a source of strength for friends, family, and colleagues during difficult times, which helps build stronger and more meaningful relationships.

Ultimately, resilience plays a crucial role in personal growth, success, and overall well-being. It allows individuals to face adversity with courage, bounce back from setbacks, and continue moving forward in pursuit of their goals and aspirations. This is because you will always be tested in life. It's time for me to share how I was tested.

CHAPTER 7

The Haunting Consequences of Our Past

The Daily Routine. My Daily Discipline. On October 27, 2020, I was engaging in what I was committed to, my daily discipline. Early in the morning, I was on the way to the gym to get in, of course, my workout that I needed before beginning work that day. But that day wouldn't turn out how I thought it would.

I made a huge mistake when I decided to drive to the gym that day while wearing my AirPods, the newer ones with noise-canceling features. While making a left turn at an intersection, unbeknownst to me, an individual on a bicycle hit the back end of my car and broke their pinky. Not realizing what had just occurred, I continued on to my high-intensity interval training class.

This period in my journey with physical fitness had become more rigorous, especially with my high-intensity interval training. These workouts tested my limits immensely. I couldn't wait to get there, but I truly had no idea what had just occurred. Days later, I found out about the incident after receiving a call from the police department because my license plate was easily identifiable.

As a personal injury attorney growing my business and using social media as my platform, I would have certainly given my information had I known someone hit the back of my car. In fact, I called my insurance company immediately to report the incident, informing them that if the individual had any injuries, it was undoubtedly my fault since I had my headphones in. My insurance company wasn't pleased with this. I soon found out that the individual had a lawyer representing him. I called that lawyer multiple times but received no response. I sent an email letting them know I had reported the claim, told my insurance company I took full responsibility, and disclosed all of my policy limits, as this is an important aspect of our job as personal injury attorneys. I expressed my hope that he gets everything he deserves.

Little did I know that despite providing all this information, the attorney handling the case decided to write a letter to the Attorney Registration and Disciplinary Commission. This wasn't even a basis for reporting. I was involved in a car accident; it was an accident. There was no ethical or professional violation because of it. But that wasn't my main concern.

I was struck with the fear of God, knowing what had occurred from 2016 to 2018, the years of my addiction. I immediately googled attorneys and looked for the most prominent firms that handle these types of issues, and I explained what happened.

I didn't tell the lawyer what was going on between 2016 and 2018 on that initial call. I told him I got into a car accident, that it was claimed to be a hit and run, but I was wearing my headphones and didn't know what happened, and immediately provided all the information necessary, not only to the police, but to the attorney. And then they still reported this. He assured me that there was no basis and that he would get this investigation shut down immediately. In three days, he did.

But there was a problem. There was still something pending, an investigation that was never closed. In 2018, I moved offices from 1 East Wacker Drive (the first office space that I had) to 150 North Michigan Avenue. The pending investigation involved the deposit of a stop-payment check related to a client's personal injury case settlement, and here's what happened: State Farm Insurance Company issued two checks for a client case. One was sent to my previous office address at 1 East Wacker Drive, and the other to the new address at 150 North Michigan Avenue.

The reason for issuing two checks was that I never received the settlement on behalf of my client and informed State Farm of this. They indicated that the original check was sent to our old office address and would issue a new check to our new address. They did so.

However, the problem arose because the check sent to the new office address had a stop payment placed on it. In the personal injury world, we must deposit settlement checks into an IOLTA account, a trust account, to safeguard our clients' settlement funds. If an issue arises, such as a check bouncing, it is automatically reported to the Attorney Registration and Disciplinary Commission without any action from the law firm. The bank automatically reports it so they can conduct an investigation, as a bounced check from a trust account should never occur. This is always the case, and I was well aware of that.

Back at that time, I received a letter from the ARDC requesting a response regarding the bounced check. I immediately reached out to

State Farm and was informed that they had put a stop payment on the check sent to the new office address. The check sent to the old address, which I still had not received, was the one they had intended to, but mistakenly did not, put a stop payment on.

I immediately requested written confirmation of their mistake. They provided the necessary documentation, and a response was given to the ARDC. Since then, I had not heard back from the Attorney Disciplinary Commission, and I believed the inquiry regarding that issue was resolved.

Fast forward to 2021, the incident involving the car accident in late 2020 had turned into something far greater. I received a response from my attorney after he obtained closure from the ARDC regarding the traffic incident. However, there was something else.

They were looking to further investigate that pending 2018 matter. I was informed that they would be subpoenaing all business and bank records, as there was an investigation pending that had never been formally closed.

I told my lawyer everything. I told him what occurred from 2016 to 2018. I didn't hold back. My addiction, my overdose, my attempt to take my own life, my disorganization of client files, spending settlement funds for costs, and other cases just to be able to keep the office moving forward. Wrong. Unethical. Not allowed. Despite the lack of clarity I had and my attempts to move my office forward, there was no justification or excuse for my actions. I knew that, which is why, immediately following my sobriety, I took steps to rectify the situation. I got things in order. I did so well before any hearing or disciplinary action. My attorney informed me that because the investigation was never closed, the ARDC had decided to conduct a full audit of my law firm. This audit would uncover what I already knew: that from 2016 to 2018, the years of my addiction, overdose, and suicide attempt, I committed ethical violations. It's that simple, and I took ownership of it.

I knew I had a substance abuse problem, not just because of an ER visit or a two-day stay at a rehab center, which now, in retrospect, is a complete blur. It was evident from the alarming amount of medication I was receiving from pharmacies. But I knew this issue would be perceived as more than just a case of being under severe mental pressure, suffering from a mental health issue, addiction, and substance abuse. I was aware that people might think this was an excuse, that it's not actually a disease.

My commitment to myself and my second chance was unwavering; I would not be swayed by the thoughts or judgments of others. I didn't care because I knew it wouldn't serve me. I was aware of how far I had come, the difficulty, the effort, and the relentless commitment to myself and my law firm that had brought me out of the darkest and worst period of my life. I understood that my purpose in making an impact on others in the area of substance abuse, particularly in the legal industry, which is rife with addiction, outweighed any shame from this investigation.

My response to the investigation was to immediately take ownership. I didn't want to waste anyone's time. I knew what it was: I had failed, I had faltered, and I needed to take accountability. These are the lessons I've learned since 2018. At the time of this filing, I am four years past it. I have found strength and stability in my dedication to physical fitness, health and nutrition, and my business. I was proud of how far I had come and grown. The impact I was building through a social media platform as a young attorney trying to grow his business by explaining and providing information about substance abuse, mental health issues, and educating in the area of personal injury law was significant. There was nothing for me to hide, so why would I try?

I knew I wouldn't. I instructed my attorney to keep this simple. To own it. I thought that would work to my benefit. And I believe it did in some aspects. But an ethical violation is an ethical violation. As attorneys, we are responsible. We must maintain and comply with those ethical obligations, even if mental health, substance abuse, or disease impacts our abilities. I know that. The investigation led to a complaint, one that was very public.

I remember the call with my attorney the first time he told me all my bank records were being subpoenaed, and I said, "I'm turning in my license. I don't want this to be so public. I know that they're going to file this. I'm going to be exposed. I've already overcome this addiction. It's been over four years. Why am I having to deal with this again?" I was truly closing shop. I don't want to deal with the shame, the embarrassment, the ridicule. And frankly, the one thing that I believed would be the only result that would come from this. My law firm, my career, anything about being a lawyer, that was over.

Immediately following, my depression took over me. After everything, how was it that this car accident would result in the return of the haunting consequences of my addiction? The irony, the frustration, and the anger that followed. There wasn't even a client complaint to the ARDC because I took every step after my overdose to fix the issues. *The consequences of my addiction were back to destroy me,* I thought. Initially, I thought this, but again, I remained committed to the second chance I was given. I shifted my mindset from allowing my thoughts and fears to dictate my response and made a promise that even in the face of adversity, I would persevere with the tools I built over the last four to five years.

My lawyer helped remind me of this after I told him I would simply turn in my law license. No matter my growth and what I'd overcome, none of that would change such a public stain on my licensure and my future career. My attorney said, "Absolutely not. You've come too far. You've done a podcast in 2019 discussing all of these mental health issues. You've garnered national news attention in your efforts on cases involving sexual assault, police brutality, and have taken steps to operate your law firm in the way that it should be. If you didn't, there would be violations beyond the time of your addiction. We both knew there was not.

The investigation uncovered some unresolved issues with files from the period of my addiction. However, each case was addressed diligently. Following my overdose, I was committed to organizing my office and preventing any recurrence of these issues. I took responsibility and rectified the situation. By the time of the hearing on this investigation, every issue had been resolved, most several years prior. Despite having medical records substantiating my addiction, this did not excuse the ethical violations that had occurred.

This broke me to my core. In the moments that followed the filing of the complaint, I was publicly humiliated by these failures, shunned by certain professionals, and removed from professional organizations where I held positions of authority. One organization, which I won't name, was one to which I became deeply dedicated. Immediately upon rejoining, I opened up about my addiction and substance abuse problems and expressed my desire to lead the Community Outreach Committee, focusing on mental health and substance abuse in the legal industry. I became the co-chair of that committee. My efforts led to being featured on the front page of the Chicago Daily Law Bulletin for organizing an event with one of the head psychologists of AMITA Health and myself. The event included a yoga session and a talk therapy Q&A where I shared my story of prescription medication abuse and overdose. However, that front-page headline led some prominent lawyers to email the organization, demanding my immediate resignation. I felt broken and defeated, knowing the amount of work, effort, and commitment I had put in over the last four years.

Those feelings were temporary because of the commitment and promise I made to give myself a second chance. Those feelings were temporary because of the promise not to let external pressures or inner thoughts control my behavior. I stepped away from the organization as it was in their best interest and continued to focus on growing my practice. I did not want my past to be a distraction to an organization I admired. I continued to utilize my social media to discuss physical fitness, mental health, and the law. That dedication, that relentless pursuit to overcome the challenges of my addiction, and my commitment to making the most out of my second chance allowed me to grow. To grow more than I ever had before at a time when I was supposed to fail. When everyone told me, your law firm is over.

Then, I remembered the response to this investigation was mine to control. That response would determine my outcome. While I cannot control, and as you will see, am not able to influence the punishment that will ultimately be recommended, I am in control of my response and actions regarding this investigation. Instead of obsessing over the unknown, the "what if," and, most importantly, what is not within my control, I chose to focus on the daily disciplines that guided me out of rock bottom.

I also knew that I would not allow this haunting time period to control a negative outcome. Instead, I knew this was another opportunity to make an impact in the space of substance abuse. I created a company called Resilient Recovery to assist individuals who are struggling with addiction by offering physical fitness routines as a means to maintain sobriety and overcome addiction. I offered insight based on my firsthand experience in using fitness as a means to overcoming prescription medication.

Even more, it is well known that the legal industry is burdened with professionals who struggle with addiction, given the stressful nature of the profession. I chose to embrace my past. To discuss my struggle so openly to inspire and potentially give light to someone going through what I had suffered.

Again, I implemented the daily discipline and standard I was committed to and saw the immediate benefits and returns. I took it one step at a time. I remained committed to the principles that I set following my second chance at life. The principle of separating the stressors and external pressures of my personal and professional life. The requirement is to have balance in dedicating time to my professional career without the two of them negatively impacting the other. That was the stability and balance I found in my second chance.

But there I was in my head again, being tested again. Thinking to myself, *This fucking addiction, again. Why? I fixed these issues. Are you kidding me? The law firm is finally growing. My social media platform started being my largest source of business.*

Even after this investigation, I remained committed to my success. 75% of the cases we were getting at this point were coming just from social media. I was embracing the media, the press. When I would sign a big case, I became strategic in my marketing skills, reaching out directly to local news stations to report on cases that I believed deserved public attention, ones that frankly got national news attention.

Well, if you put yourself out there, you can be sure that if you fail, or if there's something negative to be said about you, it will be said. This was when my resilience would be tested. How resilient would I prove to be?

There was a lesson, the main lesson of this book: External pressures and internal thoughts will not dictate my conduct. My commitment, the standard I have set for myself, and the daily disciplines I follow will remain constant, no matter the adversity I face.

I chose to be strong. I chose immediately after the filing of that complaint to do two episodes as "Part 2" of the podcast I recorded in 2019 discussing the filing of that complaint. I wasn't going to let simple legal terminology determine my character, my standards, who I was, and what I stood for. No, I was going to give a real, raw, authentic account of what it really was, what it really is. Without concern for the judgment of others, because at the end of the day, I know, and you've been told throughout this book, that your future, the consequences of today, can only be determined by you.

And there it was, the ultimate test that led to the most enlightening period of my life. It was when I discussed the benefits of physical activity—of testing your limits, pushing your capacity, and discovering just how capable you really are when you put yourself under pressure. This pressure allows those efforts or tests to expand the boundaries of your capacity.

Here I was again, being tested. In the public sphere of the legal industry, the attorneys who pay attention to these ARDC investigations, including those I had worked with and those with whom I had sat on committees, did not believe I deserved to continue being associated with any professional organizations. There was no concern for my health, well-being, or what I had overcome. I was completely ostracized. Any impact I sought to make in the sphere of mental health, addiction, and substance abuse in the legal industry and beyond was deemed irrelevant. Some of these professionals, whom I had not spoken to in years, sent emails and letters to ensure I would no longer be associated with the legal community.

These external factors and influences created an immense amount of stress and frustration. I found relief in engaging even more in physical activity, sometimes two times a day, just to release the mental anguish I was experiencing. I became even more committed to my mental well-being, physical fitness, nutrition, and, more importantly, to ensuring my office would continue to grow. The truth is, those individuals were just noise, distractions from allowing me to reach my full potential. More importantly, the judgment, fear, and stress stemming from the shame within the industry would continue, irrespective of what I knew to be true. Frankly, proving myself to others, as I learned, was irrelevant to my outcome.

The beginning of the ARDC investigation was no small matter. I thought it would be resolved quickly, especially since I admitted to all the allegations against me and had taken measures in 2019, 2020, and 2021, before the hearing on my case, to ensure everything was in order. Once the ARDC had the power to investigate, they could obtain every bank account record. However, the time period they focused on remained consistent, confined to the years of my substance abuse issue. I was aware of that, but I had made myself so publicly visible, not just in my cases, but also on my social media platform.

Initially, at the beginning of the matter filed in June 2021, I was told that the proceedings would be completed within a year or two. In the first year that followed, I began to doubt my future. I started posting less about my law firm on social media. But, as time went on and the proceedings continued with delays beyond my control or request, I decided to become even more committed to expanding my law firm. This is part of the process of truly owning a second chance at life. It's part of understanding that life is not linear and that the only thing within our control is our response to adversity.

Even with this realization from my overdose, I struggled to take full control and found myself being affected by what I thought I was in control of, what I learned. The standard I implemented to overcome my abuse of prescription medication was tested, and again, I learned. I learned no matter the adversity, even when you believe you have come out of rock bottom, you will continue to be tested. Your efforts and what you desire may be called into question, but if you remain in control of your response and committed to an unwavering discipline in mind and body, your outcome will be determined by you.

I didn't know if the ARDC wanted to make an example out of me, given the growth and exposure from social media. I was more frustrated that my addiction, and my efforts following my overdose, were all questioned; all of it was doubted. This crushed me. In reality, I should have never taken it personally.

Frankly, none of that matters. What matters is how I would embrace the second chance I was committed to. Would I allow this to break me, or would I allow myself to persevere? It took some time to understand that again. It required me to reflect on just how far I'd come. I remained focused, dedicated, and committed to the space of being an advocate for substance abuse awareness. A single Instagram post led to a Navy Lieutenant Commander sending a message asking if I would fly to San Diego with Joe, the trainer I had spoken to you about before, to give a speech on mental health and substance abuse to Navy men and women. What an honor.

We flew to San Diego. We were able to visit and tour the USS Bunker Hill in a way that nobody had access to. And after, I trained US Navy men and women by engaging in a high-intensity interval workout that Joe and I had known so well. One that we experienced together. That was awesome. I was empowered despite all the stress from this investigation.

Still, the investigation did not progress as quickly as my attorney initially told me it would. It dragged on, consuming a great deal of time. During those months, filled with fears and doubts following the filing of this complaint, I was holding myself back. I decided to step away from my social media presence. All the marketing, information, and resources I was providing on my platform, especially regarding the law,

I felt I had to stop. I thought it best to minimize exposure about this issue and to just resume once everything was resolved.

As time went on, I was reminded of my commitment and made a decision to continue persevering. In fact, I became even more dedicated to marketing myself as an attorney, recognizing the growth I had achieved from where I started and what I had overcome. I refused to let shame and regret dictate my behavior. And what was supposed to be my biggest, most detrimental experience, one that could have crushed any opportunity for my law firm to succeed, did not.

I grew even stronger, increasing my platform on social media by utilizing three aspects of my life that I knew were critical for me to share. Three aspects that were authentic and real: physical fitness, mental health, and the law. I still share these three things on a daily basis.

The haunting consequences of my past were scrutinized and doubted because of this investigation. I was required to undergo a three or four-hour forensic analysis conducted by a doctor selected by the Attorney Registration and Disciplinary Commission. I was interrogated about my substance abuse, my suicide attempt, my recovery—a recovery that didn't include a full detox stay at a rehab facility, nor ongoing engagement with a mental health professional or talk therapist following my overdose. The latter is something the industry, at least for psychological and psychiatric purposes, generally deems necessary for any recovery.

However, my experience was different. I was in a completely different place, stronger physically and mentally than ever before, due to my dedication to physical fitness. But this did not align with what the textbooks say or explain. And now, I was being judged for not engaging in what was perceived as necessary, based on a 3-hour interview. While I agree that talk therapy is an important part of the process, the benefits of physical fitness for mental health cannot be understated. This is not because I am a medical professional, but because I witnessed it, experienced it, and understood it from my actions. No one could convince me otherwise.

What most people don't understand about an addict, one who has gone through substance abuse and suffered from this disease, is that there's a lingering fear. It's the fear that when you're tested, stressed, or unwilling to face reality, you recall how easy it was for a prescription pill to offer an escape. That's why I never wanted a mental health professional back in my life. I didn't want the stresses of life, the external pressures that we all naturally experience, to lead me back to a place where I might ask a doctor for a prescription. That was a genuine fear.

Whether anyone else understood it or not, I knew that I feared succumbing to that, especially given the gravity of what was before me: the potential loss of my law license and my firm, everything I had overcome, and the responsibility of caring for my parents, which I was now embracing. I was able to buy their house for them. Through my hard work, I saved our childhood home. I achieved things I thought were impossible, and I did it all without talk therapy. I created a platform called Resilient Recovery with Joe to advocate for those currently or previously struggling with substance abuse. We promote physical fitness as a means to inspire, encourage, and build confidence in individuals who need to face life's realities head-on, not by masking, avoiding, or escaping through a pill or substance, but by confronting them directly with physical fitness providing the tools to do so.

I chose to be inspired by my strength and resilience to endure rather than to collapse and declare it over. The haunting consequences of my past did not destroy me; instead, they empowered me. They tested the limits of my resilient nature and increased my capacity to withstand adversity. That is the essence of resilience.

CHAPTER 8

The Standard of Resilience

The investigation with the Attorney Registered Disciplinary Commission remains pending and has taken longer than anticipated. So much so that I made a decision that the standards, daily disciplines, and commitments that I made to myself would be what decided my actions moving forward. I would not let the consequences of that which is not in my control disrupt the disciplines that have built the character and determination that has led to my rise from rock bottom.

I know there are certain things I can control and others I cannot. I chose to remain in control of the daily disciplines that led to my growth. I chose to persevere. Instead of hiding and being ashamed, I embraced and went further than I had ever gone before. Instead of succumbing to that not within my control, I remained motivated by my purpose and consistent in my daily disciplines relating to my health, fitness, nutrition, and business.

Remaining disciplined when dealing with issues that are beyond our control is the standard of resilience. Building that standard is important for several reasons:

- *Maintaining a positive mindset*: By staying disciplined, we can develop a positive mindset that allows us to focus on finding solutions and not dwell on the problems. This allows us to approach challenges with a clear and rational mind.

- *Managing emotions*: When faced with unexpected and uncontrollable issues, it is common to experience negative emotions such as frustration, anger, or stress. Discipline helps us to regulate these emotions and prevents them from clouding our judgment or leading to impulsive actions that might worsen the situation.

- *Making sound decisions*: By remaining disciplined, we can think rationally and objectively about the situation. This enables us to make informed decisions that are in our best interest and brings us closer to resolving the issue.

- *Protecting our well-being*: Discipline ensures that we prioritize our well-being, both mentally and physically, when dealing with setbacks. By staying disciplined, we can take care of ourselves, seek support, and engage in healthy coping mechanisms to deal with the challenges effectively.

- *Building resilience*: Remaining disciplined during challenging times helps us build resilience, which is the ability to bounce back from setbacks. It teaches us to adapt, learn from our experiences, and continue moving forward, even when things go wrong.

Discipline empowers us to take control of our reactions, maintain a positive mindset, and make rational decisions when faced with issues that are beyond our control. It enables us to navigate difficult situations with resilience and ultimately come out stronger on the other side.

In December 2022, I took advantage of an opportunity at a legal seminar focused on the use of social media in law practice. On the first night in Atlanta, I met someone who would become a mentor and inspiration in my relentless pursuit to overcome adversity—Ben Newman.

He reinforced the results that come from a relentless pursuit of setting a standard and creating a set of daily disciplines that pave the way for greatness, measured by daily effort. Despite my efforts before December 2022, I continued to struggle with allowing my feelings to dictate my behavior. I admit that, although temporarily, I let my feelings disrupt the disciplines I had implemented to overcome my struggles. I recognized that whenever I became distracted from that standard, I would falter.

With practice and time, I now understand that I won't struggle with these external influences and internal thoughts moving forward. Growth is hindered only when you fail to remain committed to the standard you set.

I had never met Ben prior to this seminar, but we quickly developed a friendship founded on similar ideologies and a relentless commitment to overcoming adversity while utilizing physical fitness as a tool to empower capacity. The day following our initial encounter, I asked Ben if he wanted to join me for a workout at five in the morning before seminars were scheduled to begin. Ben was there as a speaker. We worked out in the freezing cold outside of the Westin Hotel in the parking lot with no weights, just our bodies. A testament that there is no excuse not to engage in physical activity daily to strengthen your physicality.

During that time, I informed Ben of my story, the same story you have already been told. That allowed us to develop a connection and remain connected to this very day. I shared the story of my ethical violations and pending investigation, and he inspired me to embrace that story even more than I had before. In those moments, I became emboldened to tell this story and turn tragedy into an opportunity to make an impact on others.

In the months that followed, the effort and consistency to the standard that I implemented following my overdose increased. The limitations that bound my physical activity and mental stamina changed as my capacity to endure changed. The potential to grow from failure is measured beyond the lessons learned from those experiences. Ultimate growth from failure comes from sharing the lessons learned and serving those around you, your community, friends, and family by making an impact that could make a difference to those around you.

To realize your full potential, you must test your physical and mental limitations. Here's why:

- *Self-discovery*: Pushing our limits allows us to explore and understand our own capabilities and strengths. This self-discovery can lead to personal growth and a better understanding of ourselves.

- *Overcoming obstacles*: Testing our limitations helps us build resilience and develop problem-solving skills. By pushing ourselves past our comfort zones, we learn how to handle adversity and overcome obstacles that come our way. Something that is inevitably part of life.

- *Building confidence*: Achieving new milestones and surpassing our previous limitations can boost our self-confidence and belief in our abilities. It helps us realize that we are capable of more than we initially thought, more than we limited ourselves to.

- *Improved performance*: By constantly challenging ourselves, we can improve our physical and mental performance. Pushing our limits physically can lead to increased strength, endurance, and overall fitness. Similarly, pushing our mental limits can enhance cognitive abilities such as focus, memory, and problem-solving skills.

- *Adaptability*: Testing our limits helps us develop adaptability and flexibility to deal with different situations. It prepares us to face unexpected challenges and to think creatively when faced with new, unfamiliar circumstances.

However, while it is important to test our limitations, it is equally important to do so in a safe and healthy manner. This is essentially true for those who have struggled with substance abuse or find themselves to have addictive tendencies and behaviors. I know this far too well despite my overdose, as there were moments when I became obsessive with my fitness efforts. The physical strain resulting from a lack of rest also impacted my mental state. I was hard on myself if I didn't manage to work out every single day, sometimes even twice a day.

In those moments, I failed to recognize that the stress I was placing on my mind and body stemmed from inherent addictive behaviors that prevented me from acknowledging the importance of rest. This is why it's crucial to listen to our bodies and minds and not push ourselves beyond a point where it may cause harm or excessive stress, even when engaging in healthy habits or activities.

I've incorporated that into my life as I continue to learn from the consequences of my actions and, more importantly, the changes in my responses that serve to benefit aspects of my life that I remain in control of.

The foundation I created after 2018, from the standards I set, the disciplines I incorporated daily, and the efforts I consistently engaged in, has revealed and continues to reveal my full potential. The same can happen for you. Building this standard of resilience prevents you from allowing external pressures and internal thoughts to control your responses in ways that hinder reaching your full potential. Commitment combined with focused discipline enables one to persevere regardless of the adversity faced.

I witnessed this firsthand, despite the difficulties and adversity, more than five years after receiving my second chance at life. In fact, my law firm grew larger than ever before. My social media platform also expanded significantly. In a single month in 2023, when I was warned that my office would be destroyed and shut down, we grossed more revenue than the entire year of 2022 combined. While the road ahead remains challenging, the consistent effort and relentless pursuit to overcome obstacles became the basis for this growth. All this occurred because of the standard I set and my relentless dedication to persevering in the face of adversity. Moreover, despite public scrutiny, the law office has grown not only in revenue but also in the number of employees, attorneys, and caseload.

Staying true to my values and allowing authenticity to prevail over adversity also helped grow my social media presence. I would be lying if I said it was easy, or that it hasn't been difficult, or, most significantly, that I haven't struggled. But there is still light and hope, all of which I created and continue to create through the standard to which I remain dedicated—the standard that allows me to control how I respond to adversity. This understanding is critical for those who are currently struggling.

As I write this book, I can unequivocally admit that I am currently struggling with the consequences that will come from the ultimate decision of the disciplinary case. No matter the outcome, I will be prepared to endure and even thrive because of my preparation and dedication to overcoming this obstacle no matter the outcome.

Why? Simply put, I can only control what is in my control. I control my responses, my actions, and my preparation for what is certainly going to occur. I accept the consequences of my actions. I am accountable for my failures. I am responsible for the self-inflicted harm caused by my addiction. With that said, I know all too well that this is a disease. I know all too well the behavioral changes, the impact on one's mental state, and decision-making caused by addiction because when I finally found clarity, my behaviors immediately changed. My decision-making was and remains consistent with what is required of me, not only professionally, but personally.

The way society often addresses substance abuse and mental health issues is, sadly, reactionary. We shouldn't wait for a tragedy to strike before having conversations about mental health and substance abuse. This story aims to counter that societal failure by advocating for proactive discussions and the sharing of experiences related to substance abuse and mental health issues while one is still struggling, before a tragedy or hitting rock bottom occurs.

I have fought to keep it together for myself, not as a show or to prove anything to anyone. The truth is that it hurts, both mentally and physically. I am sharing this current adversity because I understand it all too well. I have been in such a dark place where there was no light. Sharing the struggle as it happens is a different concept. It is much easier to talk about struggles in hindsight because one has already endured them, as I once thought in the months leading up to this ethical investigation. However, the problem with this reactionary approach to mental health and substance abuse is that it perpetuates judgment and shame, leading to silent suffering. For these reasons, I choose to share.

For those who are currently struggling, the story of overcoming adversity, when told in hindsight, does not resonate. Excuses are always made. Differences in circumstances are used as an excuse not to overcome what is currently happening or causing angst. The reality is that life is not always what it is perceived to be. Even those like myself who have overcome adversity are not immune from encountering difficulties, hardships, and adversities in life.

The moments of adversity may jeopardize all that was previously overcome. It is in those moments that the standard of resilience will be tested. The capacity to withstand adversity will depend on the commitment you must maintain. When you maintain that commitment with a relentless effort and determination to persevere, you not only overcome, but you become stronger in mind and body.

I sat through four days of hearings over several months, reliving my past and being questioned about the changes I had implemented since then. I waited anxiously for the decision of the hearing board to be released. On July 12, 2023, the hearing board's recommendation was publicly announced. They suggested that I should be suspended for one year and undergo a two-year probation period afterward. I was grateful for and respected the time and considerations they had made.

Still, I felt disappointed and pained. I had made changes in my life—physically, personally, and professionally—and spoke about these changes in an effort to be a voice on substance abuse, suicidal ideation, and mental health, not because I was forced to, but well before any investigation began. This spoke to my credibility, which was recognized by the hearing board. Even so, more than five years after my overdose, I must continue to persevere and take control of what I can.

The day the recommendation was publicly announced, I was about to fly out of the country for a relative's wedding. I opened the email just before boarding the plane and collapsed. I thought I had done everything possible. I had become an advocate in this space and displayed a level of dedication to physical fitness that very few have. Despite my fears of ever talking to someone who might prescribe medication, I was recommended to engage in talk therapy.

I learned that talk therapy was very helpful in my process and continues to be so to this day. It is a tool that reminds you of the benefits of your growth, encouraging you to talk through your issues directly, not just over or under them, but confronting them head-on and delving deep into your mind to understand your behaviors.

I've always believed myself to be an intuitive person, understanding why I behave in certain ways. However, I was required to dig deeper than just my days of substance abuse, going back into my childhood to understand my behaviors. I was even told that I might be channeling my addictive tendencies into physical fitness and that I should be mindful to prevent it from becoming unhealthy. These are important lessons.

I became more focused and more attuned to my nutrition, especially given the stress I was experiencing. Observing the growth and changes in my physique, I wondered if there was internal damage that could be healed in ways beyond just physical fitness. I began exploring fasting. This would be a pivotal change in my physicality, mentality, and mental state. I learned about the process of fasting for extended periods while maintaining the same rigorous physical activity as before, which would allow my body to rejuvenate.

It was a different type of fasting than your typical intermittent fasting routine. This fasting method was backed by science, focusing on the effects of extended water fasts while maintaining the same level of physical activity I engaged in daily. The goal was to eliminate toxins and dead cells that had never been addressed because my body was primarily focused on burning the energy from the calories I consumed each day. I learned that there is healing in this process that could actually make me stronger. While still maintaining a rigorous physical fitness routine, I delved deeply into this subject. So, I took on a challenge and decided to do a four-day fast, consuming nothing but water and still maintaining the same level of physical activity I had always done. This tested my mind, not my physical state, but my willpower. There was nothing more empowering. I not only reached the best physical state I thought impossible, but I also grew stronger. That resilience I built prepared me for the letter I received on July 12, 2023.

I didn't believe my body could withstand a water fast for longer than 24 hours, but my first attempt led to a successful 96-hour fast. It was a euphoric experience. Extended fasting is unique in that it aims to repair damaged cells in your body, ridding it of dormant toxins. While it leads to weight loss, the most significant benefit was psychological, enhancing my limits, capacity, and boundaries to endure, all while continuing with a vigorous fitness routine. My first 96-hour fast involved water only, literally just water.

Day 1 was manageable because my mind was strong, and I was determined. Then came Day 2, where I encountered fatigue and hunger pains. I doubted my ability to continue, and my resolve was truly tested. But I remained determined, and then, suddenly, a shift in mindset changed everything. Days 3 and 4 brought more focus, mental clarity, and energy than I thought possible. I felt like I could go longer and test myself even further.

Beyond weight loss, the different stages of extended fasting lead to benefits such as cell repair, longevity, and anti-aging. There are several stages in this process. The first, of course, is the fat-burning stage, but the most crucial is the autophagy stage. This is when your body cleans out damaged cells, breaking them down and recycling their components for energy and new cell structures. I am not a medical professional, but this is not only what I learned but also what I felt and witnessed.

This was critical to my process because I knew my addiction had caused significant damage to my body. I sought rejuvenation and cell repair, and wanted to rid myself of the toxins I had once consumed. That was the physical aspect of it, and the results were evident within four days: I had dropped 9 pounds. In the days that followed, I gained about 3 pounds, likely due to water weight. However, the weight wasn't my main concern. The fitness routine that I maintained allowed me to not only continue reaching my ultimate physical potential but also gave me the willpower in both mind and body to push beyond the limits to which I had previously confined myself.

The psychological effects of this type of extended fasting were empowering. It was an enlightening experience, and I began to incorporate it regularly into my weekly schedule. To this day, I still include a 24 to 36-hour fast each week. I put my body through these tests while maintaining discipline in my fitness routine, building mental strength by forcing myself to deal with and manage physical strain and stress in ways that further strengthened my resilient nature.

I told myself, *I can't change this, but I can change how I respond.* And while I was feeling depressed and sad, a call of reassurance came, reminding me that it could be worse. I reassured myself that I was in control of getting through this. *You'll remain committed, as you have before, and it will be okay.* The truth was that July and August of 2023 were absolutely miserable. I was severely depressed, even though I tried to hide it.

I tried to put on the best face I could while abroad that summer. But when I returned home, I realized I was facing the hardest month since my overdose. With the investments I had made into technology and the expansion of my law firm, growing from an office of two employees over the last eight years to one employing seven, I became terrified and chronically depressed.

What was I going to do? How was all of this and that decision going to allow me to move forward? And in that month, I failed myself. I failed because I allowed my inner thoughts to control my behavior.

The ultimate test of the second chance, of the discipline I built from embracing that second chance, was in that month. I saw myself deteriorate. I didn't see myself working out in the way that I was so committed to before—I felt alone. I was in my head. Every day, I would go to work, but immediately upon returning home, I'd curl up in a ball, consumed by my thoughts. Suddenly, the paralyzing pain that I experienced from 2016 to 2018, the pain that led to me falling in my apartment, hitting my head on my desk, splitting it open, and being rushed to an emergency room after an overdose, felt as if I had time-traveled.

It was astonishing how quickly all those same pains manifested themselves. But then, a moment of enlightenment came from my business partner Anthony's wife, Bianca, just weeks before we were to travel to Italy for their wedding, where I was to be the best man.

Anthony was sitting away, enjoying the sun, and we both had our feet in the pool when Bianca turned to me and asked, "What's wrong? I know something is wrong." My friends all knew what was going on. I mean, I had put it all out on social media anyway, but she noticed a change in my behavior. Despite my internal struggles and feelings of depression, this time, I didn't completely cut out my friends and family like I did back in 2016 to 2018.

I felt more alone in August, but my friends were aware of what was happening. They pushed me, checked in on me, and were there to protect me. I admire them for that. So when Bianca asked me directly, I didn't just respond with the story of the investigation. I poured my soul out and brought it back to the same time period I began this story with—the call from the front desk about a sheriff there to serve me with eviction papers.

By the time that conversation finished, I was crying. But I turned to her and said, "Thank you. That was so cathartic." I was reminded of what I had already overcome. I recalled that no matter the adversity I face, what I have come out of, the lies that I've owned, and the second chance I embraced, have proven myself to be capable, determined, and committed. Suddenly, those feelings of anguish and depression were replaced with feelings of empowerment and pride. I got out of my head and reflected on my growth and the actions I had committed to.

I remembered that life is not linear and external pressures and inner thoughts will always test our lives. That moment of enlightenment by the pool was critical to my progress moving forward. To me, in my relentless pursuit of embracing a second chance, I must remain committed. Formidable in the face of adversity. I was reminded that those principles and the daily discipline I've maintained for the last six years are what have gotten me to where I am today. That's what it takes.

When the decision from the hearing board was released, naturally, the newspapers wanted a comment. My lawyer called me and said, "I would never advise a client to make a statement, but since you often put yourself out there, do you want to respond?"

I replied, "Absolutely." I'm not hiding behind shame and regret. I'm not hiding from the accusation of misappropriating client funds. I knew the truth, no matter how anyone might try to spin it. I understood what I had gone through. I recognized that my substance abuse, the disease I suffered from, and my lack of clarity and disorganization, while not excuses, were things I owned, rectified, and learned from.

I know who I am because of who I say I am, not just through words, but through action. So, I drafted a statement to be issued by my attorney: *"Mr. Fakhouri appreciates the opportunity to consider the Hearing Board's recommendation. He remains determined to overcome the difficulties caused by his past substance use, and he will continue to share his experience in an effort to stress the importance of mental health in the legal profession and beyond."*

That statement is a testament to my control. I know that, even in the face of adversity, my response is within my control, as is the impact I can make on others who struggle, especially in the legal field. Taking control of my life for reasons beyond self-service, but rather to serve others, is a lesson I am obligated to share. It's important to help prevent those who are struggling or have struggled from reaching rock bottom as I once did.

No matter the consequence, I know that lawyers, young and old (or any profession for that matter), who face adversity may also cope by turning to substance abuse. The reality is that addiction does not discriminate, and it is only exacerbated by social media. In a professional context, social media has enabled my growth, but it also demands constant attention, a truth I am well aware of. I adapted my law practice to meet the demands created by my efforts on social media. This reality, coupled with the economic stress and familial pressure that initially led to my addiction as a coping mechanism, and substantiated by evidence of a mental breakdown and medical records, as well as my unrelenting commitment to my physical and mental well-being, will not alter the consequences I must face. That is something beyond my control.

What is in my control is my continued recovery. What is in my control is my standard of resilience. I will persevere because I will maintain the discipline necessary to overcome adversity. That discipline includes a commitment to engaging in daily physical activity, engaging in talk therapy, and maintaining stability through consistent effort. This is what it takes. This is how you build your standard of resilience.

Irrespective of this disciplinary action, I choose to persevere. I choose to provide light to those who may be similarly struggling. I choose to discuss the troubling issue of mental health and its effect on professionals, especially lawyers because my personal experience requires me to. I made that decision.

My silence would send a chilling message to those currently masking their struggles and fearful of coming forward due to the potential loss of their profession. I believe we need to convey a message of compassion and understanding to young and older lawyers alike. We need to encourage them to come forward and confront their issues, assuring them that our system won't punish them but will provide resources to support their recovery. I told myself that even if the industry wouldn't do it, I would.

There I was, becoming more resilient than ever, more focused, and more dedicated, not only to my physical fitness routine but also to my mental health routine. Talk therapy is a very important part of the process, one that has helped guide me through this test of my second chance.

I am a firm believer that with the right therapist and by confronting your issues head-on, you will persevere. In the months following my conversation with Bianca, I made changes and continued to persevere. The opportunity to tell my story was now presented to me. Writing this book and embracing my challenges to enlighten, inspire, and make an impact on others became my new motivation. That is the standard of resilience.

This is how you strive for greatness despite adversity. Reflecting back on August of 2018, I could have never envisioned myself to be where I am today. I did not believe that I was capable of such growth. I did not believe I was capable of repair. The proof came from my action. The proof came from my relentless dedication to taking each day one at a time and, at the very least, accomplishing the tasks I had set as part of my daily discipline.

Time revealed my strength. Patience enabled me to carry on. Resilience gave me the strength to persevere in the face of ongoing adversity. You must understand that no matter the adversity, no matter what you're going through, even if you think you've moved past it or believe you've overcome it and it's just a distant memory, life will continue to test you.

You may even be tested, as I was, with the haunting consequences of substance abuse nearly six years later. True power is built through the ability to endure. It is strengthened when you break through the boundaries of your perceived limitations. The litmus test of your capacity is determined by your ability to overcome failure or difficulty and to continue persevering in the face of adversity. The more you overcome, the stronger you will become. It's that simple. It's all within your control.

The key to achieving your goals, reaching your ultimate potential, and testing the limits of what you can endure, requires action. It's about the choices you make, the commitments you undertake, and the daily discipline you implement in both mind and body. Focusing on physical activity in a way that serves you, transcending the bounds of physicality into mentality, will provide the tools you need to get through.

These will be the sources of the resilience you need to persevere. Embrace your challenges. Deal directly with your issues. Set a standard and make a commitment to yourself. A commitment that incorporates daily discipline in mind and body through fitness, fasting, and talk therapy. The relentless pursuit to persevere is for you to decide. The actions, decisions, and responses you commit to daily are within your control.

In the end, life itself, the lies we tell ourselves, the rock bottom we may hit due to those lies, and the second chance we may be fortunate enough to receive, are ours to control.

Embrace your power. Implement daily disciplines to build a stronger, more resilient you. Give yourself a second chance.

CONCLUSION

A Strong Mind

You are now equipped to develop the skills necessary to realize your full potential. Implementing daily disciplines in both mind and body will naturally build the mindset required to remain resilient and persevere in the face of adversity. Deciding to give yourself a second chance at the life you desire requires accountability. It involves recognizing the lies you tell yourself that prevent you from confronting the realities of your circumstances. It means no longer hiding, masking, or avoiding the struggles you face, and instead dealing directly with the obstacles before you.

You must find what motivates you to remain determined and relentlessly committed to your goals. Remember, you can only control what is within your control if you truly want a second chance at life. Do not let moments of failure, fear of failure, or single events in life dictate your future potential. When you commit to incorporating disciplines that strengthen your physical and mental capacity, you develop the skills necessary to create a standard of resilience that enables you to persevere in the face of life's inevitable challenges.

If you've been given a second chance at surviving as I was, now is the time to take advantage of the opportunity to make the most out of life. To do so, never forget the following:

- *Reflect and set goals*: Take a moment to reflect on what truly matters to you and what you want to achieve in life. Setting meaningful goals can give you a sense of purpose and direction.

- *Embrace gratitude*: Appreciate the second chance you've been given and practice gratitude in your daily life. Being grateful for the little things can help shift your mindset to a positive and optimistic outlook.

- *Live in the present moment*: Focus on the present moment and fully engage in the activities and experiences you encounter. Avoid dwelling on the past or worrying too much about the future. Mindfulness practices like meditation and talk therapy can help with this.

- *Prioritize health and well-being*: Take care of your physical and mental well-being. Eating a balanced diet, exercising regularly, getting enough sleep, and managing stress can positively impact your overall health and energy levels.

- *Pursue your passions*: Identify the things that bring you joy and invest time and energy into pursuing them. Whether it's a hobby, a creative outlet, or a career path, follow your passions and incorporate them into your daily life without fail.

- *Cultivate relationships*: Surround yourself with positive and supportive people who uplift and inspire you. Build and nurture meaningful relationships with family, friends, and loved ones, as they can contribute significantly to your overall happiness.

- *Expand your horizons*: When you test your limitations, you increase your capacity. Continuously learn and grow by exploring new interests, acquiring new skills, or expanding your knowledge. This can help you discover new passions, broaden your perspective, and make the most out of your second chance.

- *Give back*: Consider volunteering or engaging in acts of kindness to contribute to your community or those in need. Helping others can bring a sense of fulfillment and make your second chance even more meaningful.

Remember, making the most out of life is a personal journey, one that only you can control. It requires you to define what is important to you. Stay true to your values, do not hold yourself back due to moments of failure, embrace new opportunities, and seize each day with gratitude and enthusiasm.

THANK YOU FOR READING MY BOOK!

Scan the QR Code to Access Some Free Resources

I appreciate your interest in my book, and value your feedback as it helps me improve future versions. I would appreciate it if you could leave your invaluable review on Amazon.com with your feedback. Thank you!

www.ingramcontent.com/pod-product-compliance
Lightning Source LLC
Chambersburg PA
CBHW030242010526
44107CB00030B/1304/J